WINNING IN CHINA

FOR IRINA,
WE'VE HAD A LOT
OF GREAT ADVENTURES
IN 中国. LOOKING
FORWARD TO MANY
MORE!

XO,

LELE SANG AND KARL ULRICH

WINNING IN CHINA

8 STORIES OF SUCCESS AND FAILURE IN THE WORLD'S LARGEST ECONOMY

WHARTON
SCHOOL
PRESS
Philadelphia

Published by Wharton School Press
The Wharton School
University of Pennsylvania
3620 Locust Walk
300 Steinberg Hall-Dietrich Hall
Philadelphia, PA 19104
Email: whartonschoolpress@wharton.upenn.edu
Website: wsp.wharton.upenn.edu

Ebook ISBN: 978-1-61363-107-2
Paperback ISBN: 978-1-61363-108-9

Contents

Introduction
If Amazon Can't Succeed, Can Anyone?

When Amazon CEO Jeff Bezos visited China in 2007, three years after his company entered the market, Amazon was already one of the two leading players in Chinese ecommerce, with 12% market share—not far behind Dangdang's 18%. Bezos expected that one day soon China would be a double-digit percentage of Amazon's sales.[1] Yet, by 2019, Amazon, the most powerful and successful ecommerce company in the world, had quit China.[2]

If Amazon can't win in China, can anyone?

The overarching theme of this book is winning in China, the world's largest economy. By 2025, China is likely to be the world's largest economy by any measure.[3] However, in terms of population and purchasing power parity, it is already the world's largest economy.[4] In roughly 40 years, a brief interval in most economies, China vaulted from productive anemia to economic might.

Any firm considering entering China is motivated primarily by one factor: the demand for goods and services from about 1.4 billion people. A foreign firm hopes to profit either from directly slaking that demand or, in the case of business-to-business (B2B) companies, from serving other companies that eventually touch consumers in places as diverse and far-flung as Beijing, the country's capital, and Xi'an, once the Chinese terminus of the storied Silk Road.

Entry is only a first step: For profits to be realized, the company must possess and maintain resources that give it a competitive advantage. We call these resources *alpha assets*, and they include proprietary technologies, distinctive capabilities, recognized brands, and lower costs (chapter 1). Success elsewhere doesn't guarantee that a company has these assets in China, as the country presents beguiling different challenges than other countries.

In this book, we answer four questions:

1. Which factors explain the success or failure of foreign companies entering China?
2. What challenges and pitfalls can a company entering China expect to encounter?
3. How can a prospective entrant realistically assess its chances?
4. Which managerial decisions are critical, and which approaches are most effective?

Why We Wrote This Book

The original idea was sparked by Lele's disappointing experience with LinkedIn after she returned to China from the United States. She had been an avid LinkedIn user in America, using it regularly for news, career opportunities, and, most importantly, networking. She would reach out to school alumni, people she had met, or strangers whose profiles piqued her curiosity to connect with them and sometimes become friends or collaborators.

Yet that experience hadn't been re-created in China. Few Chinese professionals on LinkedIn showed interest in her attempts at networking. She tried to reconnect to a former colleague with whom she had lost contact and got his response a full year later. His explanation: "I'm happy with my job. I don't normally go on LinkedIn." They then connected on WeChat, China's dominant social media app, and never communicated via LinkedIn again.

A year before Lele's return in 2014, LinkedIn officially expanded into China. As in each of its markets, the company positioned itself as "the professional networking" platform and pitched this idea hard. Yet seeing the lack of interest among her fellow Chinese in networking through LinkedIn, she doubted whether the firm was on the right path. (LinkedIn is featured in chapter 5.)

LinkedIn was not the only foreign company that concerned Lele, a former journalist who had reported on multinational corporations in China. There were others, including the company she worked for. She often found herself bogged down in unnecessary late-night conference calls with her US colleagues, being asked to implement strategies that didn't fit China, waiting for each tiny action to be approved by headquarters, and hearing customers complain about how slow her company was and how fast their Chinese rivals could be.

These encounters, along with seemingly constant news about foreign companies' challenges in China, inspired Lele to find out why foreign companies struggled so much. After she left a corporate job, she decided to write a book about multinationals' failures in China.

Then she met Karl, who had spent years researching innovation in China as a professor at the Wharton School of the University of Pennsylvania. Karl was aware of the failures, yet also saw a diverse set of foreign companies that had become successful in China. They decided to collaborate, attempting to paint a complete picture of both failures and successes. Lele is Chinese and Karl is American, but each has spent a significant amount of time in both countries, and they share an enthusiasm for a more interconnected global economy. They wrote this book with the goal of learning from the experiences of the intrepid companies that have attempted to enter the Chinese market, to help foreign companies understand the realities of venturing into China, assess their chances of success, and guide their planning and decision-making.

Why Is China Special?

China is an especially attractive market because of the size of its population and the spending power of that population. Yet China has proved more of a puzzle to US companies than other large markets, like India or the European Union. First, the Chinese government plays an outsize role in guiding the economy. Second, tacit networks and relationships (*guanxi* in Chinese) are critical to the way business works. Third, the Chinese economy continues to grow at a blistering pace, and companies operate and innovate with commensurate speed—and so must foreign companies that want to succeed there. Finally, culture and language typically present a larger obstacle in China than they do in other large foreign markets, particularly for Western firms. Put together, these attributes create a unique environment, one that is both different enough and important enough that it warrants its own analysis. What worked for an American company in Brazil won't work in China.

Defining Success

In conducting interviews for this book, we encountered both people who described failure and those who described success—and sometimes they were referring to the *same* company and events. One observer's commercial flop could be another's learning experience. Before we begin our analysis and case studies, we should be clear about the possible definitions of success and failure.

There are at least four ways in which a firm might succeed with its entry into China:

- **Positive financial outcome.** Did the company realize a return on the investment?
- **Market significance.** Regardless of financial return, did the company achieve recognition in the Chinese market? That is, did it move beyond being a niche player?
- **Organizational development.** Did its parent company become stronger and more capable as a result of its China initiative, possibly through organizational learning, innovation, or recruitment of talent?
- **Options for the future.** Is the firm better positioned to exploit future opportunities in China?

If we define success in these four ways, *failure* can be defined as their converses—as not achieving one or more of these four outcomes. Of course, in some cases, observers indulge in the all-too-common tendency to revise history: What began with a financial goal becomes a learning experience when the former goal is not achieved.

Decision-makers in companies planning entry into the Chinese market need to be clear from the outset about their expectations. We believe that most managers are not motivated to enter China just to learn, to build organizational capabilities, or to open up options for the future. They aim to *meet a significant portion of the demand in their category with sustained competitive advantage.* This is the definition of success we adopt.

Why not focus on financial returns? From a practical perspective, directly observing financial returns for a unit within a multinational corporation is not typically possible for outsiders. However, financial returns must flow from success as we define it. Any firm that meets a lot of demand with sustained competitive advantage will earn a higher than average return on invested capital.

Why Do Businesses Fail in China?

Even a cocktail-party conversation about the causes of business failure in China reveals some obvious hypotheses, and in fact some of these are good explanations. They include the following.

Government

Most naive observers quickly point to government intervention in the Chinese economy as a primary driver of success and failure. They argue that the Communist Party of China either inhibits foreign companies or favors their domestic rivals. This has unambiguously been the case in some instances. Facebook, despite impressive efforts at building relationships in China and CEO Mark Zuckerberg's enthusiasm for the country, is simply not allowed by the government to operate in China. Chinese government industrial policy may also assist foreign companies when there is a critical societal need. This is largely the story behind the automotive industry in China, which we discuss in chapter 4. But for most companies in most industries, there are few true regulatory barriers. And in other cases, the issue is more one of a company not being willing to play by Chinese rules. For instance, Microsoft offers its Bing search engine in China, while Alphabet doesn't offer Google there. This is the result of Microsoft being willing to locate its data centers in China, with Chinese government oversight.

Business Ecosystem

Partnerships and business relationships matter in any economy—but especially in China. The Chinese use the term *guanxi* to refer to informal connections that assist in getting things done. Guanxi exists among individuals in social networks but also among organizations. For instance, Alibaba's investors include Boyu Capital, a private equity firm with political clout; Citic Capital Holdings, an investment firm of state-owned financial conglomerate Citic Group; and CDB Capital, the China Development Bank's private investment arm. And Alibaba's success is rooted, at least partly, in deep political connections impossible for a foreign rival to achieve. This does not mean that foreign companies cannot develop guanxi, as Intel has done (chapter 8), but that the effort will demand careful selection of leadership and a long-term commitment to building relationships.

Product-Market Fit

Of course, the Chinese market may simply not need what a foreign firm offers. While most human needs are universal, preferences and practices are not. A foreign firm may not sufficiently adapt its products and services to the desires of its Chinese customers. LinkedIn (chapter 5) exemplified this problem.

Competition

Chinese investments require massive amounts of capital and patience, particularly in emerging categories. For instance, the transportation company Didi burned hundreds of millions of dollars *per month* in its fight with Uber in 2016. JD.com was willing to lose money for years to vanquish Amazon. Competition is not merely a question of will. The foreign firm may simply not possess sufficient barriers to domestic competition if its brands are not well known, if it lacks proprietary know-how, or if it does not enjoy significant production efficiencies.

Organizational Factors

Virtually every manager we interviewed pointed to agility—or the lack thereof—as decisive in success and failure. The Chinese economy changes at what sometimes feels like 10 times the speed of more mature markets. The extent to which a foreign firm operating in China must coordinate its actions with its headquarters abroad largely dictates its agility. The organizational structure of the unit in China, relative to the parent's, and its autonomy in the country figure in every case in this book.

Organizational factors include more than structure. The qualifications and experience of the leadership team that runs the organization also help determine success. What are the required qualifications and experience? Must leaders be native Chinese with years of experience operating in similar roles in China?

Finally, commitment can determine success, in terms of time horizon, expectations, and patience around setbacks. Intel, which is featured in chapter 8, understood it would invest for 15 years before realizing an outcome. A common pitfall is a mismatch between the hoped-for payback period and the time required for success.

How to Read This Book

We begin the book with a conceptual framework for success (chapter 1), much of which applies to any setting, not just China. The book then considers case studies of eight companies: Amazon, Norwegian Cruise Line, Hyundai, LinkedIn, Sequoia Capital, InMobi, Intel, and Zegna. Some of the cases, like Sequoia, can be considered unqualified successes, and some, like Amazon, unqualified failures. But for others, like LinkedIn, the outcome remains to be seen. We start with two companies that have exited China: Amazon and Norwegian Cruise Line. Then we consider Hyundai, which enjoyed initial success and now faces challenges. The fourth company, LinkedIn, maintains its presence in China but acknowledges that success, as we define it, has so far been elusive. We then turn to four clear successes: Sequoia, InMobi, Intel, and Zegna.

We chose these companies to represent a variety of experiences and industries. Although most are headquartered in the United States, we also include companies from Korea (Hyundai), India (InMobi), and Italy (Zegna). Some companies have been in China a very long time, and some are relative newcomers. While it is impossible with eight cases to cover the full diversity of corporate experiences in China, we hope that our sample can provide models for companies yet to enter China.

Our Sources and the Challenges of Studying Failures

The topic of success and failure of an organization is likely to be sensitive in any context, and it's even more so in China. Four of the companies we studied denied our formal requests for interviews and information. In most cases, principals still employed by companies would not agree to interviews, citing company policies. More surprising, perhaps, was that principals no longer employed by the companies in most cases would not speak with us, except on the condition of anonymity. The network of executives who have led multinationals in China is small and interconnected. Many of those we spoke to, although holding strong opinions, would not express them on the record. Yet, we were able to verify what we were told with public information, such as financial reports, employee head count, and company public actions. In researching the book, we interviewed no fewer than five insiders associated with each example, and, in most cases, many more. Additionally, we interviewed other executives, managers, researchers, and industry analysts—more than 100 in total. When possible, we quote our sources directly. In a handful of other cases, we refer to them anonymously or integrate what they told us into the narrative. We shared drafts of chapters for comment from those with direct knowledge of events. We believe that the resulting accounts are accurate. Inevitably, different individuals may have different recollections of facts or will disagree with the interpretation of those facts.

We admire all the companies we studied. They are all pioneers, regardless of what happened to them in China. Winning in China isn't guaranteed, even with a smart plan and a capable team. In fact, we believe success is influenced in part by factors that are unknowable and unpredictable. Our goal here is not to assign blame or credit but rather to describe and interpret the experiences of bold companies for the benefit of those considering entering China. History can be a teacher, and China, a country with 3,500 years of written history, has much to teach.

Chapter 1

This Is What a Business Needs to Succeed in China

Profit growth is a key objective for virtually any company, and geographic expansion can provide that growth. Consider InMobi, a start-up we feature in chapter 7. By 2010, the company had finally become a leader in advertising on mobile devices in its home market of India. Its founder, Naveen Tewari, knew India would remain a small market for mobile advertising for at least a few years. After extending its services to several smaller countries, Tewari was considering expansion to China, a huge potential prize.

The logic of expansion is that an asset developed in one place, such as product or brand, can confer a competitive advantage in another. After all, consumers around the globe share similar needs for food, shelter, communication, entertainment, and transportation. A firm that meets those needs in one part of the world should be able to serve customers in another part. However, the playbook can rarely be copied exactly. Taco Bell's Cheesy Gordita Crunch, popular with teenagers in Houston, may not appeal to those in Hunan. And the Maytag brand, created more than a hundred years ago in the US Midwest, means nothing to someone shopping for a washing machine in Shenzhen.

This book aims to guide managers like InMobi's Tewari in assessing their prospects and planning for success. This chapter presents a framework for understanding success in China. We apply the framework to each of our eight cases and, in chapter 11, show how it

Figure 1.1: Conceptual Framework for Understanding Success in China

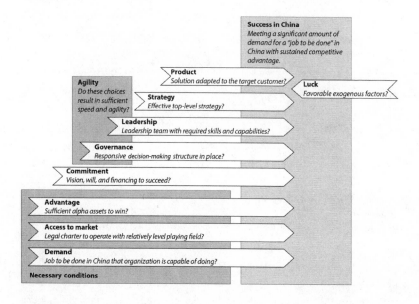

can be used prospectively. The framework, shown in Figure 1.1, comprises three necessary conditions and five managerial decisions, plus agility and luck. We treat each of these elements in turn.

Three Necessary Conditions

1. Demand

Firms exist to satisfy the needs of customers. In the language of famed Harvard Business School professor Clayton Christensen, customers hire a company to *do a job*.[1] The most fundamental requirement for success in China is that the firm sets out to do a job that lots of Chinese consumers—and the country has an estimated 328 million urban households—need done.

Nearly any need that exists in one's home market exists in China. For instance, the need to prepare and serve food at home exists in both the United States and China. Yet the need for tools *to serve ice cream at home* varies dramatically: Americans eat a lot of ice cream at home, the Chinese almost none. One of us (Karl) is a cofounder of a company in the United States, Belle-V, whose best-selling product is an ice cream scoop. Belle-V would face a quixotic challenge entering China to do the job of improving the ease of something few people do. It might fare better with an improved dumpling steamer or wok spatula.

While the ultimate source of demand in society is individual consumers, the business-to-consumer (B2C) companies that cater to end consumers also need goods and services, thus giving rise to B2B firms. Just as consumer needs can vary across geographies, so do the needs of companies. For instance, paper bank checks are used rarely in China, so a company hoping to sell check-processing equipment would likely fail. But, as with consumer needs, if the need is conceived more generally, it likely exists in China. For instance, reframing the need for check processing as the need for payment transmittal results in a job that is indeed real in the Chinese market.

A clear-eyed assessment of what job (or jobs) the company can do and whether there is sufficient demand for that job prefigures any hope of success. Just trying to foist an American offering on Chinese consumers won't work.

2. Access to the Market

In considering entering the Chinese market, a foreign firm must find out whether the planned activity is permitted by law. Some categories of businesses are closed to foreign companies. However, as of 2019, there were just 40 such categories, each defined quite narrowly.[2] Air traffic control systems is one. Some categories require a Chinese partner. For instance, degree-granting higher education requires partnership with a Chinese university and approval from the Ministry of Education. Another example is the internet, where the government often restricts investment. Yet a VIE (variable interest entity) structure can sidestep the restriction. Under a VIE, a foreign company establishes a subsidiary in China. The subsidiary signs a contract with a Chinese company, and the Chinese company invests and operates in the restricted sector. This is the approach Amazon and LinkedIn took.

Despite these restrictions, the vast majority of business categories in China are open to foreign companies, and, in some cases, an industry falls within a category that the government hopes to encourage as part of a major initiative or its Five Year Plan. For these categories, incentives may be available for foreign companies.

Three important caveats are worth noting. First, government policies are dynamic, having changed significantly at least three times since the 1978 opening. Second, policies can vary by province and city, in part because of local political power and in part because of deliberate creation of different zones with different rules for different economic purposes. Third, many policies are deliberately vague, allowing for administrative discretion in interpretation.

3. Advantage

Given a job to be done in China and a legal charter to operate, the third necessary condition for success is a potential source of competitive advantage. Competition for the Chinese market is intense. The size of its market and its surging growth aren't secrets to anyone, and Chinese entrepreneurs and multinationals from all over the world are vying for shares. Ultimately all competitive advantage arises from controlling some resource or asset that helps deliver a solution to customers and that cannot readily be acquired by rivals. We call these resources the firm's *alpha assets*.[3] Alpha assets may include efficient production systems, brands valuable to consumers, or proprietary products. For example, Intel's chip design and manufacturing technology and Zegna's brand are both alpha assets. Alpha assets are a firm's unfair advantage, required to give it a reasonable chance to prevail against local competition. By definition, they're already possessed by the firm and not easily acquired.

Five Managerial Decisions

If a company has satisfied the three necessary conditions for success (demand, access to the market, and advantage), it'll next have to make five decisions—all of which are under the control of the parent company. These decisions are made at the outset of the venture and updated as experience plays out.

1. Commitment

With ventures into the unknown, the time and money required for success will usually be greater than expected. In China, the prize is large, and investors have been willing to place large bets. These factors make the commitment required to succeed in China larger than for any other foreign market. In some cases, firms fail to realistically forecast the costs required and lose enthusiasm once reality proves more expensive than their projections. In other cases, the initial commitment of resources is just too stingy, leading to the worst possible outcome: wasting resources with no hope of a payoff. Of course, smart commitments can be contingent and can grow as milestones are achieved.

2. Governance

The structure and administration of the relationship between the China unit and the parent organization is a key managerial decision. On the one hand, the unit could operate mostly independently, like a start-up. On the other, it could operate more like a regional division, little different from other divisions around the world. The full range between these extremes is possible, but most of the companies we studied are somewhere in the middle. Specific governance decisions required include the following:

- To whom does the top manager in China report?
- Which decision rights does that person have? How significant are the decisions that require consultation with headquarters?
- Which resources (e.g., R&D, marketing, finance) are replicated in China, and which are located at headquarters and shared?

These decisions depend on the business context. For instance, Intel is unlikely to replicate the development of semiconductor-fabrication processes in China, because that activity requires deep expertise about the physics of manufacturing, which does not vary by geography and which benefits from a single global center of excellence. In contrast, LinkedIn China would be unlikely to share a marketing department with its US counterpart, because acquiring customers in China differs from acquiring them in the United States. To a large extent, a parent company's choices on these matters reflect trust and the willingness of the parent to accept the risks associated with trust.

3. Leadership

There is considerable debate and academic research about the extent to which CEOs of large companies really matter.[4] There is no such debate about start-up CEOs. Any venture capitalist will tell you that the three most important factors in venture success are the team, the team, and the team. And leading a foreign company's entry into China more resembles managing a start-up than stewarding a division of a big company in a mature market. Yet managers unfamiliar with the parent company's culture will struggle to marshal resources they need or win support at headquarters for their plans. The skills needed to excel as a manager within a large firm may even be at odds with those needed in a new venture—savvy corporate politicians are seldom also resourceful pioneers. Add to this mix the need for someone who's comfortable operating in both China's business environment and that of the parent company. The number of people who have all these skills is tiny, though growing, and most companies will have to compromise on at least one of these desirable qualities.

4. Strategy

If a firm has a clumsy strategy, it will likely stumble, even when it enters a booming market with a strong commitment and capable leadership. In this context, we intend "strategy" to refer to the top-level plan for entering the market and achieving sustainable success. Typically, this strategy can be described in one or two sentences. For instance, for Hyundai, one of our focal cases, the strategy was this:

> Enter China in a 50–50 joint venture with Beijing Automotive Group and offer a highly affordable car for the Chinese middle class using an existing design, an existing component supply chain, and a Chinese assembly plant. Use this approach as a stepping-stone to building the Hyundai brand in China and to offering more upscale models in the future.

Hyundai's strategic alternatives could have involved different partners, different initial market segments, and different approaches to design and production. Although plans inevitably evolve and companies must adapt, the top-level strategy usually guides the company for the first year or two of its China venture. Getting it right is not a straightforward exercise or a guarantee of success; efforts in China will be buffeted by a host of uncertainties: actions of competitors, macro trends in the market, unexpected decisions from policymakers, and plain dumb luck. Still, trying to enter China without a well-planned local strategy is like trying to hike in a trailless forest without a map and GPS.

5. Product

For a given job to be done, various solutions might be offered. Consider the need for clean clothing each day. You might buy a washing machine, tote dirty clothes to a laundromat, or even rent outfits, as has long been done with tuxedos and is now an option with expensive designer outfits. A company achieves product-market fit when its solution is preferred by the consumers it aims to serve. In practice, this fit can be influenced by consumers' price sensitivity, their cultural norms and preferences, and their alternatives. For instance, in the United States, clothing washers and dryers are almost always separate appliances. In Europe, given much smaller homes, they're often combined into a single unit. But in China, which also has small homes and high energy prices vis-à-vis most families' budgets, apartments often have a semi-enclosed porch or a balcony on which clothing is hung to dry. A plan to sell full-size washers and dryers in China would almost certainly fail.

In B2C markets, most solutions require significant adaptation to meet the needs of the Chinese consumer. But there are instances of nearly identical solutions working globally. These are often technical or narrow in their scope, such as with microprocessors or industrial adhesives. But in a few interesting cases, a product's main benefit may be its foreignness, as seems to be true of Starbucks. In most cases, the needs, preferences, and tastes of Chinese consumers vary enough that firms hoping to succeed in China must adapt their offerings. Most companies have the capability to do this, so doing it is mostly a question of willingness to localize and expend the cost and effort required.

Emergent Factor: Agility

Managers of foreign companies in China cited one factor more often than any other in our discussions: *agility.* The Chinese market operates at the speed of an online marketplace, with offerings, prices, and even vendors changing constantly. Established companies are more accustomed to markets that function like shopping malls, where change happens more slowly and someone can't just rush in, set up a kiosk, and start selling something new. In China, competitors respond to opportunity in days, not months or quarters, and startups backed by abundant venture capital sprout up. Established firms, even in their home markets, tend to be cautious. Add to that the complexities of coordination across oceans, time zones, and organizational boundaries, and they are considered sloths in comparison with China's cheetahs. Unfortunately, agility is not itself a single managerial decision. Rather, it emerges from other managerial choices, particularly the governance of the China unit, its leaders, and the autonomy they're granted.

A central tension limits agility for foreign companies in China. The greatest agility would arise from appointing an entrepreneurial leader and giving that person complete autonomy. But that structure would then mirror an independent start-up, leaving little, besides perhaps funding, for the parent to contribute. The premise of foreign investment in China is that the foreign firm brings alpha assets. Tapping into those assets requires coordination with headquarters.

Luck: What You Can't Control

Economists don't like the word "luck." They lump it into a category they call "exogenous factors," which basically means everything outside your control that affects you. No matter which word you choose, the reality of randomness can't be changed, but it can be prepared for. The first step is acknowledging that exogenous factors can be divided into *known unknowns* (e.g., the precise level of the exchange rate between the renminbi [RMB] and the US dollar over the next five years) and the *unknown unknowns*. By definition, the "unk-unks" aren't listed in advance, but retrospectively most companies would identify the arrival of the novel coronavirus in 2019 in China as an unk-unk. To some extent, firms can prepare contingency plans or at least calculate the chance of success with some assumptions about the likelihood of the known unknowns. For a start-up, the timing and nature of competition is a known uncertainty, for which responses can be planned in advance for a reasonably small number of scenarios. But the unk-unks are different; scientific breakthroughs, terrorist acts, social movements, and macroeconomic crises are in most cases scenarios so unexpected that trying to articulate and plan for every one of them is not a productive use of managerial attention.

Every Success Factor Brings a Potential Failure

For every success factor, there is a complementary way for a firm to fail in China. For example, a company can mistakenly believe that its global brand will entice Chinese consumers. In these kinds of cases, the failure may have been avoided by a more realistic assessment of consumer tastes and the market. We hope to provide a diagnostic instrument for such assessments in chapter 11.

Other failures stem from missteps and can be avoided through better managerial practices. Bias and arrogance can be mitigated with a deeper knowledge of China and its challenges. Missing key needs of customers can be mitigated with more careful and honest research into the job the firm hopes to do. Delivering a solution that meets its customers' needs can be achieved by adapting global products for the Chinese market or designing new products specifically for that market. Errors in execution can be avoided through a clear-eyed assessment of the resources needed to win and by putting in place skilled executives with the autonomy to act with agility. Our case studies in the rest of the book illuminate both pitfalls and their costs, as well as some of the ways in which successful companies have recognized and managed these risks.

Chapter 2

Amazon
The Flywheel Stops Spinning

When Bezos stepped off a colorfully painted Indian truck in Bangalore in a white Nehru jacket to hand over a "surfboard-sized" $2 billion check to Amazon's Indian unit chief,[1] China had fallen out of his favor. That was 2014, 10 years after Amazon entered China. Though the Chinese ecommerce market was then much bigger than India's—nearly 80 times larger in 2014—it had never received a similar investment from Amazon. In fact, in the prior 10 years, the ecommerce giant had gone from being a leading player to an afterthought. In 2016, when Bezos announced an additional $3 billion investment in India,[2] his China business had shrunk to just a 1.3% share of the country's ecommerce market.[3]

By 2019, Amazon was gone, having closed its China domestic ecommerce business—a rare defeat for one of the world's most admired companies.

An Early Toehold

In 2004, when Bezos first eyed expansion into China, Amazon was still known as mostly an online bookstore. It had established operations in the United States, Canada, France, Germany, Japan, and the United Kingdom. The Chinese ecommerce market was just taking shape. Internet users had grown to 87 million,[4] and the B2C online transactions reached 4.2 billion RMB,[5] the official currency in China (about $512 million at the time). The market's potential had already lured eBay, which a year earlier had acquired EachNet Inc., a Chinese online auction site. To fend off eBay, Jack Ma, founder of Alibaba, had launched a consumer-to-consumer retail site, Taobao, to sell products ranging from cosmetics to electronic components. Another entrepreneur, Richard Liu, whose brick-and-mortar stores had suffered from the 2003 SARS epidemic, had shifted to ecommerce in 2004. His online offering would eventually become JD.com. But amid all of this early jockeying, two Chinese companies already stood out: Dangdang and Joyo.

Founded by the former Wall Street consultant Peggi Yu and her husband, Guoqing Li, in 1999, Dangdang was the biggest online bookseller in China. It had been inspired by Amazon: Yu had returned to her native China and established a similar venture there. In 2003, *The Economist* dubbed Dangdang "China's Amazon."[6]

Joyo, for its part, started in 1999 as a site for downloading software onto desktop computers. Its founder, Jun Lei, who would later start smartphone-maker Xiaomi, reconceived it as an ecommerce site selling books, music, and videos. "There was a popular book titled *Business the Amazon.com Way*," said Gang Yu, a former vice president for Amazon China and founder of Yihaodian, an online grocery store later acquired by Walmart. "Lei read that book and literally followed that book to build Joyo."[7]

Amazon courted Dangdang first, offering $150 million for a majority stake. That offer was rebuffed by the husband-and-wife executive team, who insisted on keeping majority ownership themselves. Amazon then turned to Joyo, which accepted $75 million for a complete acquisition. Bezos was satisfied. "We're happy to be part of one of the world's most dynamic markets," he said.[8] So began the Amazon era in China. Eventually, the company, named after the largest river in the world, would learn that China's Yangtze River was every bit as treacherous as its namesake Amazon—it turned out that the former was filled with fierce "crocodiles."

Amazon's initial plan was to integrate Joyo into its China team. But that didn't work. The Joyo team, consisting of Chinese entrepreneurs and professionals, faced requirements that they use English in the workplace and write narrative memos in preparation for meetings, a quirk of Amazon's corporate culture. Even more challenging, their vision for the company differed from Amazon's. The divide delayed annual planning. By the spring of 2005, Amazon China still hadn't developed a strategy for the year. That April, seven months after the acquisition, the president and the vice president of Joyo.com were gone, soon followed by the rest of the original team. Amazon replaced many of them with Western-educated Chinese professionals returning home, a practice employed by many multinationals entering China. Hanhua Wang, a Motorola veteran with a doctorate in psychology from the United States, became president. The two vice presidencies were taken by a former operations director at YesAsia .com, a Hong Kong–based online retailer, and a former investment banker from International Netherlands Group.

Joyo.com then embarked on Amazon-ization: From the website to logistics, everything was replicated from Amazon global. A template developed elsewhere would dictate operations in China. After all, that template had powered Amazon's global expansion. There was no reason to doubt its effectiveness. Yet the Chinese market soon deviated in vexing ways from the global norm.

Amazon had leveraged a *flywheel model* to drive growth in each market in which it operated. Here's how that worked: A great customer experience brought traffic to the website. That traffic attracted more third-party sellers to the site. Third-party sellers brought more products, and that further improved the customer experience and customer traffic. In a second important cycle, the growth associated with the flywheel allowed Amazon to achieve greater scale and reduce its unit costs. It then passed along those lower costs in the form of lower prices, which further delighted customers.

To spin up the flywheel in China, Amazon aimed to improve each underlying factor. It expanded Joyo's offerings to cosmetics, consumer electronics, toys, baby products, and other categories. It promised "everyday low prices and authentic goods." It migrated its advanced IT systems to China, which enabled better analysis of transaction data and better prediction of demand, so as to better manage inventory and reduce delivery times. It invested heavily in logistics, building fulfillment centers in major Chinese cities.

Acknowledging the unique challenges of China,[9] Amazon did make some local adaptations. One that Yu, the former vice president, remembered was refining the website. According to Yu, the first website, in imitating Amazon global, attracted almost no traffic. The China team had to make adjustments. With each iteration, the site became "longer and messier." Though that departed from Amazon global's simple and clean style, it fit Chinese customers' tastes. The team then experimented with personalization. They divided customers into four categories based on two variables: male versus female and new versus existing. They displayed different pages to the different categories. That move doesn't seem impressive now, but back then, in a fledgling ecommerce market, it was radical—and effective. "That increased our conversion rate by 17%," said Yu.

Amazon China was also a pioneer of digital payments. When cash-on-delivery was common, Amazon China introduced a mobile point-of-sale system, with its couriers carrying a device for customers to pay via credit or debit card. All of those efforts paid off. For the first few years following the acquisition, Amazon was a leader in China's ecommerce market.

Aggressive Upstarts

Though Amazon was progressing, an upstart was already trying to undercut it. In 2007, JD.com, an electronics retailer, received a $10 million investment from Capital Today. JD's founder Liu, who had grown up in one of the poorest parts of China and had only recently learned the term "venture capital," had originally asked for $2 million. But Capital Today saw more potential than even Liu did. The two agreed on strategy: JD would pursue market share, costs be damned. The company thus embarked on a transformation from consumer electronics retailer to full-service online retailer. More categories meant more customers—and more revenue.

Another new player, Alibaba, also aimed to thwart Amazon's dreams of domination. Ma, Alibaba's founder, had started out trying to compete with eBay; he'd founded Alibaba back in 1999 as a B2B marketplace site. Worrying that eBay would come after Alibaba's wholesalers, he set up Taobao, meaning "searching for treasure," as a defensive move. Knowing eBay charged users listing and transaction fees, Taobao announced free listings and transactions, which attracted sellers and buyers. eBay's China chief, Yibo Shao, disparaged the approach, famously quipping, "Free is not a business model." But Taobao stuck with it for five years, fueled by a portion of the over $80 million it raised in 2004 from Softbank Capital and others.

In the early days of ecommerce in China, one of the biggest obstacles to attracting shoppers was a lack of trust. Taobao addressed that with an instant messaging tool, Aliwangwang, and a third-party online payment solution, Alipay. Aliwangwang connected buyers and sellers, allowing buyers to ask questions before purchasing. This kind of interaction was discouraged by eBay, but it helped persuade people to buy.

Alipay redoubled that trust. It temporarily held purchase funds until the merchandise was accepted by the buyer. This practice was rapidly adopted by Taobao users, even as PayPal, eBay's payment system, failed to take off in China.

By the end of 2006, eBay had shuttered its China site and formed a joint venture with Tom Online, a Beijing-based internet company. By then, Taobao had 30 million registered users and an 80% share of the consumer-to-consumer ecommerce market, with sales of 16.9 billion RMB ($2.06 billion at the time).[10] Two years later, Taobao launched a separate B2C site Taobao Mall (Tmall), expanding into Amazon's territory.

As customers flocked to JD, Taobao, and Tmall, Amazon's flywheel became harder to spin. As it had in the United States, Amazon opted to open its Chinese marketplace to third-party sellers. But many Chinese sellers weren't interested.

Since there can be multiple sellers on Amazon offering an identical product, Amazon developed the "Buy Box" to help *the buyer* select the best option. The box is the rectangle in the upper-right corner of the product page, where the buyer can make a purchase directly by clicking either "Add to Cart" or "Buy Now." If a buyer searches for a pair of men's Puma Tazon 6 FM running shoes, the product page will display a Buy Box next to a vendor selected by Amazon. Beneath the Buy Box on the page are other options. But most buyers won't bother clicking on them or even notice them, so most of Amazon marketplace sales are made via the Buy Box. As a result, capturing the Buy Box becomes each seller's goal. Which seller wins the Buy Box is decided by an Amazon algorithm based on a variety of factors, including price, the seller's customer rating, inventory levels, and fulfillment methods. The *vendor* can't buy the Buy Box. Sellers must learn the rules, improve their service, and win the designation. This comports with Amazon's "customer obsession" principle: Award the box to the best sellers that give customers the best experience.

Other ecommerce players in China didn't use a buy box. Instead, if the same buyer went to JD or Taobao for the same pair of shoes, he or she would get pages of listings from many sellers. That's obviously not as convenient for buyers, who must winnow the options, but it's friendlier to sellers. On other sites, sellers could also buy ads to push their rankings higher, improving their chances of being picked by a buyer. As a result, many sellers exited Amazon, choosing instead to sell through Taobao and JD. Yet Amazon's executives in China didn't think they could banish the box. "If you do that, you wouldn't be Amazon anymore," said one former executive who spoke on the condition of anonymity, citing the sensitivity of the subject.[11]

Apparel was one of the weakest categories on Amazon China's site. Popular brands favored by Chinese consumers, such as Zara and Uniqlo, were not available—but were on Tmall. The reason, according to a former senior manager who also spoke on the condition of anonymity, was that Amazon wasn't willing "to give preferential policies to those high-profile brands, even though recruiting them would attract more customers and significantly boost the site's traffic."[12]

Amazon wouldn't even cater to its most important seller. Xinhua Winshare Publishing and Media Company was the biggest merchant globally at Amazon in terms of the number of orders. Yet Amazon rejected Xinhua's request for a commission discount if it reached certain sales goals, said the same manager.

Price Wars

Other parts of the flywheel also malfunctioned. Amazon's low prices, which had served the company well for years, were threatened by competitors' price wars. Richard Liu had continued raising capital. By the time JD went public in 2014, it had raised $2 billion. Thanks to its cash trove, JD could initiate price wars to draw in customers at the expense of margins. It attacked Dangdang, announcing all of its books would be 20% cheaper than those of competitors. It invaded brick-and-mortar retailing, aiming to take down Suning and GOME, its main rivals in home appliances.

Dangdang, Taobao, Suning, GOME, and other ecommerce players all responded with discounts of their own. The price wars attracted media attention and boosted JD's sales and notoriety. At the time, Dangdang, which went public on the New York Stock Exchange in 2010, couldn't risk its profitability to grow market share. Its cofounder, Guoqing Li, thought the price wars would end soon enough because JD seemed to be squandering its money. But JD kept pulling in new capital. In retrospect, Li said: "Richard is so lucky. Investors gave him $2 billion to burn."[13]

Pricing wasn't the only way competitors outfoxed Amazon. Alibaba's Ma created a shopping festival on Tmall, Singles Day, on which he offered large discounts and promotions to attract new customers. Singles Day began as a way for singles to celebrate being single on November 11. (It came to be referred to in China as "double 11.") Ma turned it into a shopping phenomenon. The first Singles Day was November 11, 2009, when 27 brands offered discounts on Tmall. The one-day sales reached 52 million RMB ($7.64 million). Sales surged in the ensuing years: 936 million RMB ($138 million) in 2010, 5.2 billion RMB ($813 million) in 2011, and 19.1 billion RMB ($3.03 billion) in 2012. By 2019, Singles Day sales had hit 268.4 billion RMB ($38.3 billion). That's more than $30 billion *in one day*. Other e-retailers cashed in too as Singles Day became a national phenomenon, but Tmall and Taobao were the biggest beneficiaries. Imitating Ma's approach, other e-retailers offered up their own festivals. JD.com created the 618 festival, Sunining.com created the 818 festival, and Vipshop created the 128 festival. The numbers refer to a month and day and involve the auspicious Chinese numeral 8.

Amazon responded to neither the price wars nor the shopping festivals. In an interview with Reuters, Hanhua Wang, the head of Amazon China, said that, in his calls with Bezos, their discussion centered on the Chinese consumer, not the company's performance. "We tend to take a very long-term view of things," Wang said. "Amazon's China race is not a sprint but a marathon."[14] With rivals willing to lose money to gain share, did Amazon have the financial endurance for a marathon? "It's a common practice for Chinese start-ups to burn cash to acquire customers and secure market share," said Yu, the serial entrepreneur whose portfolio included two ecommerce companies, Yihaodian and 111.com.cn. "If I don't burn money now, I won't have a chance because everybody is doing so to grab customers. If I wait, the customer acquisition cost would soon double or triple." Though Chinese entrepreneurs clearly saw this pattern, US companies were slow to change strategy. Years later, Diego Piacentini, former Amazon senior vice president for international retail, who had overseen operations in Asia and Europe, said the company should have spent much more in China: "On everything."[15]

The Logistics Battle

One area in which Amazon established an early advantage over its Chinese rivals was logistics. The company invested heavily in warehouses and other infrastructure. By 2012, it had 11 fulfillment centers, more than its rivals, and those centers' combined size was nearly 500,000 square meters, the biggest Amazon network outside of the United States.[16] For a long time, Amazon's logistics network led its executives to believe that no one could match its ability to make speedy deliveries. But soon enough, JD's Liu figured out how to do just that.

In 2007, Liu decided to expand JD's offerings from electronics to general merchandise. He made a bold bet on building an integrated logistics network that combined warehouses, fulfillment centers, and last-mile delivery, something that even Amazon US wasn't doing at that time. Back then, China's delivery industry was chaotic—a bunch of small companies scattered in different regions of a large country. There was no equivalent of UPS or FedEx. Packages often arrived late or damaged. Half of JD's complaints related to deliveries. In addition, cash-on-delivery, the payment approach JD adopted, was risky. JD relied on the delivery companies to collect money, but couriers sometimes grabbed the cash and disappeared, causing big losses for JD, which relied on sales of high-priced electronics.

To solve these problems, Liu aimed to, in effect, combine the services of an Amazon and a UPS in a single company. It was a costly bet and one that was widely questioned, both inside and outside JD. Even years after the giant logistics network was up and running, Ma was publicly predicting it would fail and take JD down with it. (Ironically, Ma would later invest billions of dollars to build its own logistics network.) But Liu's bet would eventually become a commanding advantage for JD. "Amazon has a great logistics network," said Long Wong, former director of supply chain and transportation at Amazon China. "Compared to its rivals, it rarely makes mistakes. But Chinese customers definitely value speed more than anything else."[17]

JD also approached distribution differently. Amazon shipped orders nationally. When something was out of stock in one warehouse, Amazon would pull it from another and ship it to the customer, regardless of that person's location. For example, if someone in Beijing placed an order and only the warehouse in Shanghai had the product, Amazon would ship it from Shanghai. The trade-off was a longer shipping time, but products were always available. JD, in contrast, prioritized speed. If a product requested by someone in Beijing was unavailable in nearby warehouses, it would tell the customer the product was out of stock, as opposed to shipping from more distant Shanghai. In addition, unlike Amazon, which relied on dozens of local couriers for the last mile of delivery, JD built its own delivery team, with a network of delivery and pickup stations, and drivers riding three-wheeled electric bikes. The bikes would weave in and out of the chaotic traffic in China's teeming cities and venture onto dirt roads in the country's rural vastness. Regional shipping plus an in-house delivery team provided astonishingly swift fulfillment. In 2010, JD launched same-day delivery for orders submitted before 11 a.m. and next-day delivery for orders submitted before 11 p.m., and it was free for all customers. Amazon's same-day delivery at the time was available only in the United States, and it came with a cost. Prime members, who paid $79 a year for free two-day shipping, paid an extra $6 for each item, and non-Prime members paid an additional $15.

The Flywheel Winds Down

At this point, Amazon had fallen behind in selection, pricing, and delivery. To exacerbate matters, even its website—the front door for any ecommerce company—lacked a feature that Chinese customers expected: instant messaging. Introduced by Taobao, instant messaging had been adopted by other ecommerce sites, and Chinese consumers wanted the ability to spontaneously chat with customer service reps. Whenever they had a question regarding products or delivery, they shot off a message. With a click, they were connected to someone. But in the worldview of Amazon, chat was a bandage over flawed web design—a good website should provide all the information customers needed. In addition, any service staffed by humans significantly added costs and sapped efficiency. Amazon emphasized automation. It even created a key performance indicator

(KPI), called perfect order percentage (POP), to discourage human interaction with customers. It didn't want to chat with customers. If someone contacted Amazon by email or telephone or left a message on its site regarding products, this was perceived as a nonperfect order, said the former Amazon senior manager. With this mind-set, it was no surprise that executives in Amazon's headquarters rejected the China team's request to add instant messaging to the site.

As the components of Amazon's flywheel malfunctioned, the virtuous cycle turned vicious. A more limited selection, slower delivery, and a perceived lack of customer service led to fewer website visits. Fewer visits meant reduced sales volume, which drove away third-party sellers. Fewer sellers further reduced selection, and so on.

In 2012, Amazon's market share dropped to less than 2%.[18] Alibaba and JD had risen to dominance, with 52% and 22% shares, respectively. Hanhua Wang, Amazon China's president, stepped down. Though Amazon's sales had increased from 100 million RMB ($14.2 million) to 10 billion RMB ($1.42 billion) during his seven-year tenure,[19] the growth was dwarfed by that of local rivals. After Wang's departure, Amazon repeatedly swapped out its China head.

Meanwhile, JD reached 60 billion RMB ($8.69 billion) in sales, and Alibaba's Taobao and Tmall rocketed to 1,000 billion RMB ($145 billion). They went public on the New York Stock Exchange and Nasdaq. Taobao and Tmall had become an "everything store," where consumers could find anything from a Volkswagen SUV to a dog translator. JD's distribution network has since grown to include 25 logistics parks, about 730 warehouses, nearly 7,000 delivery and pickup stations, and around 85,000 delivery personnel, covering 99% of China's population. Dangdang, Amazon's original rival, managed to eke by: It went private in 2016, and its market share has shrunk to around 1%.

Stubborn or Steadfast?

In business, as in life, there's often a fine line between being steadfast and stubborn, and it may well be a measure of luck that distinguishes the two. Get lucky, and you look smart in your resoluteness; end up unlucky, and you look dumb in your mulishness. In China, Amazon stuck with what it knew and ended up looking less like the world's largest river and more like a drought-starved trickle. "Back then, there was a strong belief that over time China will conform to the global Amazon model, because if it worked everywhere else, it must work in China," said the former Amazon China executive. "If you have patience, eventually you'll be successful. The model will prove itself."

That had happened elsewhere. An example is Japan. Amazon Japan was launched in 2000, and Japan has become Amazon's second-largest international market after Germany, with $12 billion in revenue in 2017.[20] Winning there convinced Amazon that its flywheel would work in China. Undergirding this mentality, the executive added, were Amazon's leadership principles. One of them was: *Leaders are right, a lot.* Looking at Amazon's history, it is hard to argue with this view. Bezos had been questioned, challenged, and ridiculed for many critical decisions, including the Kindle, Amazon Web Services, Fulfillment by Amazon, and machine learning. Yet almost every time, he had been right. His people naturally wanted to believe he was right again about China.

The local executives were aware of the distinctive characteristics of the Chinese market, but they had trouble making themselves heard. "Hanhua had his ideas, but he couldn't convince Diego Piacentini," said Wong, the former director of supply chain and transportation who was sent to China from Seattle after Amazon acquired Joyo. Even if the local team had been given sufficient autonomy and resources, would that have been enough to turn things around? Gang Yu, the Amazon executive turned entrepreneur, doesn't think so: "You have to be very entrepreneurial to succeed in China."

Applying the Framework

By its own admission, Amazon's ecommerce business failed in China, and it abandoned its plans after 15 years of effort. Amazon stuck to its flywheel, but in China, the flywheel fell apart.

Several decisive factors contributed to the failure:

- Amazon did not possess sufficient alpha assets in China. When Amazon entered China, it was already a key global ecommerce player and possessed alpha assets in its many markets, including its brand, its information technologies, its scale, and its vast selection of goods. However, in China, the brand was largely unknown. The technical talent was valuable but not impossible to obtain. The products offered in China, though well aligned with the tastes and needs of Chinese consumers, were much narrower in selection than Amazon's offerings elsewhere. So, the only potential alpha asset supporting Amazon in China was its logistics, which was better than that of its rivals initially. However, JD took away that edge by building its "Amazon + UPS" network.
- Amazon did not truly commit to the Chinese market, at least not to the extent that JD and Alibaba did. Its lack of commitment may have been the right managerial decision in the larger context of Amazon's business. Amazon has since enjoyed jaw-dropping returns on invested capital elsewhere, and winning in China probably wasn't worth an all-out commitment of billions of dollars. For JD and Alibaba, winning was an existential imperative, since most of their revenues came from home.
- Amazon's China unit lacked autonomy. Amazon's governance structure required most of the functional units in China, including finance and operations, to report to Seattle, impairing agility. One example was the debate over adding a chat function to the website, which consumed two years but never happened. That lack of local autonomy inhibited swift decision-making, a key component of winning in China.
- Amazon's local leadership consisted primarily of experienced corporate managers. To be sure, many of them were natives of China or had worked there.

Table 2.1: Summary of Success Factors for Amazon

Factor		Explanation
Demand	▲▲▲	Ecommerce boomed in China from 2004 to 2019 when Amazon attempted to establish a strong market presence.
Access to market		Amazon and other ecommerce retailers were allowed to operate independently in China as wholly owned foreign entities.
Advantage		Alpha assets in other markets (e.g., brand, technology, scale, and product assortment) could not overcome limited commitment and autonomy.
Commitment	▽▽	Amazon did not allocate as much capital to China as was available to its local rivals, perhaps because of better opportunities elsewhere.
Governance	▽	Amazon granted little autonomy to its China unit.
Leadership	▽	Managers were capable executives but perhaps not equipped to deal with scrappy competitors and certainly limited by the constraints from headquarters.
Strategy	▽	The strategy of replicating the "Amazon way" did not work in China, where local competitors were willing to take huge losses to win market share.
Product	▽	Limited localization may have been sufficient had price and assortment been superior to that of competitors, but this was not the case.
Agility	▽▽	Neither the governance structure nor the leadership team was optimized for speed.
Luck	▽	The tenacity and ferociousness of competitors Alibaba and JD.com was bad luck.

Note: Upward-pointing triangles indicate a positive factor. Downward-pointing triangles indicate a negative factor. The number of triangles is our subjective assessment of the relative importance of the factor. We omit indicators for those factors that we do not believe were significant for this case.

Yet their competitors were entrepreneurs—ambitious insurgents who did whatever they could to win. Exceling in a multinational company demands different skills than starting something from nothing: the former is like coaching a team; the latter like leading an expedition into an unmapped jungle. To make matters worse, Amazon's China leadership didn't seem able to exert any influence on its parent company's decisions. Richard Liu of JD once commented:

"Amazon doesn't trust their China team. . . . Ask Hanhua whether he can implement his ideas? He can't."[21]

These elements and other factors in the framework are noted in Table 2.1, along with our subjective assessment of the decisive factors.

In the next chapter, we turn to Norwegian Cruise Line, a company that made extraordinary efforts to customize its offering for the Chinese consumer—yet still failed.

Chapter 3

Norwegian Cruise Line
How "Made for China" Fails

O n a cold and humid winter day, Carol Zhao, a travel agent from Shanghai, received an invitation to a party in Miami. She flew across the Pacific Ocean and arrived at the dazzling three-story beach mansion. There, the mansion's owner, Frank Del Rio, president of Norwegian Cruise Line (NCL), and NCL's executive team were waiting for her and her peers from China's tourism sector. NCL was aiming for the booming Chinese market and planned to send a customized cruise ship there to grab a share. It thus gathered a delegation of leading Chinese travel agents, whom Del Rio referred to as "partners," and sought input from them.

Apart from NCL's hospitality, which included air tickets, accommodations, and wining and dining (rare treatment from an international cruise company), what struck Zhao most was NCL's determination. She remembered what Del Rio said: No matter how tough it got in China, NCL would work with its partners to get through it.[1] That was 2016.

Fast-forward to February 2018: Del Rio brought encouraging news at the company's quarterly earnings call, and despite a difficult environment, NCL had reported a profit. "We remain optimistic that the vast opportunities possible in China will come to fruition," he said.[2]

Yet only a few months later in July, NCL decided to move its cruise ship *Joy* out of China, just a year after the ship had arrived. The news shocked the cruise industry.

A Latecomer's "Weapon"

NCL started cruising from China in 2015. After years of planning, it set up a China branch, headquartered in Shanghai, with offices in Beijing and Hong Kong. By then, the market was crowded. Costa Cruises had entered in 2006 as the first international cruise line, followed by Royal Caribbean three years later. By the time NCL arrived, rivals had been dispatching their ships from Chinese ports for years. Undeterred, Del Rio saw advantages to being a latecomer. "It is no secret that the early entrant lost money here for many, many years because there wasn't an established marketplace," he said. "So if you're astute and observant you learn from past mistakes, and we hope to learn from past mistakes, not repeat them."[3]

One rival in particular offered a host of lessons: Royal Caribbean was intent on dominating the market. Unlike other cruise lines, which often sent smaller, older ships to China, Royal Caribbean entered with *Legend of the Seas*, which accommodated nearly 2,000 passengers, making it the largest cruise ship in China at the time. Its arrival created a sensation. Two years later, Royal Caribbean brought in *Voyager of the Seas* and *Mariner of the Seas*, both even bigger. Two years after that came *Quantum of the Seas*, a then record-breaking behemoth. Royal Caribbean bragged that the ship was longer than five Boeing 747s,[4] parked nose to tail. Coupled with its heavy spending on marketing, Royal Caribbean's China fleet set the company apart. Though it entered China behind Costa, Royal Caribbean enjoyed better brand recognition.

Inspired by Royal Caribbean, NCL set out to build a new ship that wasn't just large but also customized for the Chinese market. It was built by Meyer Werft, a German shipyard known for constructing spectacular ships, and designed to accommodate 3,883 passengers. To cater to Chinese tastes, the ship boasted special features. On its topsides was 333-meter-long artwork depicting a phoenix, designed by a Chinese professor from the prestigious Central Academy of Fine Arts. Inside, it provided suites for extended families. "You know the one-child policy," said Del Rio. "Often you have that child's parents and grandparents. So we built different cabin configurations for that kind of situation."[5] The ship had 60% more retail space than was typical, because of the Chinese people's reputation as eager shoppers. Around 50 luxury brands, including Bulgari, Gucci, Prada, and Armani, awaited passengers on board. The ship had three casinos, a laser-tag course, and the first go-kart track at sea. Other features aimed to replicate Chinese culture. These included teahouses, karaoke rooms, gaming rooms with mahjong sets, and Chinese restaurants.

NCL also tried to accommodate Chinese consumers' aversions. The Chinese, for example, are not sunbathers. So NCL reduced the size of the pool deck and turned that area into a "tranquility park," filled with faux grass and trees, where tai chi and yoga were offered.

With all of the costly customization, the *Joy* embarked with high expectations. Harry Sommer, NCL's executive vice president for international business development, called it "the premier ship in China" and predicted it would "command the highest prices."[6]

Smooth Sailing

While the ship was under construction, NCL managed to acquire a license from the Ministry of Transport in just a few months. The government in Shanghai awarded a tax reduction. The entry permit and preferential tax treatment came easily not because China wanted to curry favor with NCL but rather because of how badly the country wanted a cruise industry.

Cruising in China had barely existed before 2006, when Costa Cruises sent in its *Allegra*. Since then, the market had grown at an astonishing rate, as much as 40% annually. Between 2012 and 2016, the number of passengers surged from 216,700 to 2.1 million.[7] These passengers mainly traveled on ships owned by international companies like NCL and Costa.

Though China had mastered the construction of aircraft carriers and battleships, cruise-ship building was not among its competencies. Only in 2018 did the China State Shipbuilding Corporation, the country's largest shipbuilder, form a joint venture with Carnival to develop China-built ships. A few Chinese companies had bought cruise ships elsewhere to test the waters, but a lack of knowledge and management skills often impeded their growth. As a result, the industry remained dominated by foreign lines. "It's not enough to just have some cruise ships and salespeople to get travelers on your ships," said Weihang Zheng, general secretary of the China Cruise and Yacht Industry Association. "To run a cruise line, there is a whole system to learn."[8]

The central government had been encouraging the development of the cruise industry. Its 13th Five Year Plan had included the cruise sector, and Premier Li Keqiang had advocated for the industry several times. Local governments along the coast, including those in Shanghai, Tianjing, and Guangzhou, had built ports, improved infrastructure, and developed preferential policies in hopes of attracting cruise ships.

NCL set up its Shanghai office in October 2015. David Herrera, a senior vice president, was sent from Miami to oversee it. The company hired Alex Xiang from Royal Caribbean to lead the sales team. Xiang said he was drawn to the company's culture. "They value family," he said. "It came from Frank's Cuban heritage, and it's definitely compatible to the Chinese culture."[9] Del Rio was born in Havana and left Cuba with his family at age seven. He married his high school girlfriend, Marcia, who also had emigrated from Cuba. An accountant by training, he started Oceania Cruises with a used vessel and 20 employees—eight of whom were family members. He had grown the company into a fleet of six ships, capable of carrying 5,300 passengers, when it was acquired by Norwegian Cruise Line in 2014.[10] He then became NCL's CEO.

Xiang, reflecting on his time at NCL, believed the culture created a work environment that enabled NCL to operate flexibly and adapt quickly to changing market conditions. (He'd end up being proved right, but not in the way he imagined.) Another trait that struck him was NCL's "partner first" attitude. That came from a lesson Del Rio had learned from Renaissance Cruises' bankruptcy shortly after September 11, 2001. As the chief financial officer and then co-CEO of Renaissance, Del Rio knew the cruise line had marginalized travel agents. He now regarded them as a lifeline.[11] In China, where travel agents are responsible for over 85% of ticket distribution, that view dovetailed with market realities.

Zhao, director at China International Travel Service, saw firsthand how serious Del Rio was about cultivating relationships with agencies like hers. She recalled offering suggestions on customizing a *Joy* restaurant to fit Chinese customers' tastes. A year later when the ship arrived in China, she and her peers found that many of their ideas had been implemented. "It's hard to imagine any other cruise line would do this," she said.

To prepare for *Joy*'s arrival, NCL increased its team in China to 60 people. It also abandoned its no-ads-in-Asia policy, running spots on TV as well as posting ads in busy subway stations and elevators of high-end office buildings. It sought out endorsements from Chinese opinion leaders and became the first cruise company to use WeChat, China's dominant social media platform, to promote a cruise ship's arrival.

In a particular coup, it landed Leehom Wang, a Chinese American pop star, as *Joy*'s "godfather." Del Rio thought Wang's international profile matched the image NCL wanted to project with *Joy*, a ship designed to combine features of the East and West. Whether *Joy* achieved what Del Rio envisioned is debatable, but associating Wang with the ship turned out to be a coup. According to Zhao, with several foreign ships docked in China's ports, many customers couldn't remember either "Norwegian" or *Joy*, despite NCL's many ads. Some would simply ask for tickets to the ship where "Leehom Wang is the captain!"

For further marketing, NCL partnered with ecommerce giant Alibaba. Alibaba's mobile payment tool, Alipay, was integrated into the shops on *Joy*. This made shopping on board easier than on competing ships. Elsewhere, Chinese customers had to use either a dual-currency credit card or cash to shop, given that all the transactions were completed in dollars. NCL also offered an Alipay-only discount and did a preview cruise for 1,700 VIPs and guests from Alibaba. "Many of them were Alibaba's platinum store owners," Xiang said. "They livestreamed their journey on the cruise, great exposure for us."

NCL's cruise itineraries didn't offer quite the same level of enticement. They were limited to trips to Japan, with stops in Fukuoka, Nagasaki, Okinawa, and a few other cities. In theory, South Korea was an option. But relations between China and Korea had grown tense over the deployment of a US missile defense system in Seoul, so NCL took Korea off its destination list, as did other cruise lines. Even so, *Joy*'s early trips proved popular. "Before *Joy*'s debut, tickets for the whole summer had been sold out," Xiang said.

NCL wanted to position *Joy* as a premium ship, so prices were set high. "Ours were close to Royal Caribbean's and 10% to 15% higher than other cruise companies," Xiang said. The average price of five- to seven-day trips was between 4,000 RMB and 4,500 RMB ($570–$640), which ranked fifth or sixth among all the markets NCL operated. "Taking into consideration Chinese consumers' income, our ticket sales were pretty good."

The Ship Goes South

Everything worked well, until it didn't. After a few months of operation, NCL noticed that *Joy*'s retail and casino sales were slackening. Cruise lines in China banked on duty-free shops and gambling. Chinese travelers' love of high-end brands—Chanel bags, Tiffany necklaces, Rolex watches—is well known among retailers. Cruise lines, including Royal Caribbean and Carnival, had thus enlarged the size of their onboard stores. Royal Caribbean's *Quantum of the Seas* had once boasted the biggest shopping center, at 750 square meters, but it was surpassed by *Joy*'s 900 square-meter marketplace. *Joy*'s casinos, too, were supersized on account of Chinese consumers' reputed affection for games of chance. Gambling is illegal in China, but national laws don't apply on the high seas.

Some of NCL's offerings performed as expected. The Bulgari store broke the chain's worldwide record by having the highest average sales per unit area. "Bulgari was awesome," said Jing Lin, a 32-year-old lawyer who traveled with her husband and her parents. Lin bought a necklace there, finding it "much cheaper than buying it in China and even 10% cheaper than stores in Japan."[12] Another popular onboard shop was Godiva. Its cheapest ice cream was $5, a deal compared with the $7 someone would have paid in Beijing or Shanghai. The rest of the shops lacked appeal, Lin said. "There's no price advantage compared to shops on Carnival or Royal Caribbean. In general, most of us were just window shopping to pass time."

The casinos didn't deliver the expected results either. *Joy*'s customers were mainly middle-class people with families. Many of them had only a limited willingness to risk their money on a slot machine or card table; their gambling was strictly an amusement. "Our casino revenue was not better than other markets NCL operated," Xiang said.

Shopping and gambling revenue, though lackluster, had not been expected to be major profit contributors, and their shortfalls didn't doom NCL's plans. "The main profit of onboard consumption comes from food, beverage, and offshore sightseeing," said Xiang, "especially beverage—the gross margin could reach [up] to 85%."

Onboard dining had been designed to cater to Chinese tastes. From Chinese hotpot to Japanese sushi, French haute cuisine, and American steaks, *Joy*'s 20 restaurants promised an edible adventure. Yet most customers dined only on complimentary fare, leaving over half of the premium restaurants underpatronized. Lin and her husband had dinner at Neptune's, a Western-style seafood restaurant. It charged $48.88 per person, making it the most expensive offering on the ship. Her parents didn't join them, as they thought the restaurant too pricey.

Like any other cruise ship, *Joy* had plenty of bars, offering an array of drink styles. It's normal for a Westerner on a cruise to down six or seven drinks a day. Yet for Chinese tourists, a couple of drinks, or even none, is the norm. Culture is part of the reason. The Chinese usually drink during meals, when beer, baijiu (a Chinese liquor, similar to vodka), or red wine is served with food. Younger Chinese will drink at bars, but older, more traditional folk, who were *Joy*'s main customers, tend not to. Even Lin said she bought only three cocktails on her whole journey. The rest of the time, she either got free lemon water or used the electric kettle in her room to boil water. The kettle was part of NCL's customization: The Chinese love drinking hot water, but having access to it also gave them a reason not to buy drinks onboard.

Price was another deterrent. There's not much difference between the price of drinks onboard and off-board for Western tourists. They could buy a pint of beer at their local bar for five to seven dollars and saw similar prices on cruise ships. Yet for a Chinese tourist, five dollars could buy a substantially bigger bottle of beer at a neighborhood shop. NCL couldn't lower its drink prices because of its procurement practices, Xiang said. International cruise lines often use global sourcing for onboard supplies, except for perishables. NCL was no exception. "We could have tried local sourcing to lower the price," said Xiang, "but Miami was not willing to make an adjustment for just one ship, one market, especially [when] the result was not guaranteed." Beverage consumption became the biggest point of divergence between Chinese and Western consumers. That was critical—because, as Xiang already noted, drinks typically provide high margins.

Zhao, the travel agent, said NCL may have misjudged its potential market in China. From her experiences selling tickets to Chinese tourists, she said the majority fell into the lower-spending category. "There were luxury brands, fancy restaurants, and bars for a couple hundred high-spending tourists. But were there enough things for the vast 90%? They were the backbone of revenue."

NCL made changes to accommodate the travelers who were coming aboard. It added milk tea to its beverage menu and provided a nonalcoholic beverage package at eight dollars per day, though it required customers to buy it for their whole journey. Those changes didn't bring much improvement. NCL also considered more aggressive onboard marketing. Other cruise companies used amplified announcements to promote their products and services. Some even sent their staff around their dining rooms to pester people to buy wine with lunch and dinner. Yet those techniques didn't align with NCL's premium brand image and its global operational standards. "They were definitely not elegant," said Xiang, "but think about how Meituan or Ctrip got started and how they won. They relied on this very aggressive marketing approach." (Our Sequoia chapter includes more information about Meituan and Ctrip.) NCL clung to its standards and got stuck with the bill: "Our onboard revenue was one of the worst among all the markets," said Xiang.

Another revenue stream that trickled was sightseeing. In the West, tourists often book their off-ship excursions with cruise lines directly. The lines organize the tours and profit accordingly. But in China, this part of tourism remains in the hands of travel agencies. There is a historical reason. China opened overseas tourism to its citizens in the 1990s, when the government allowed travel agencies to organize group trips to Singapore, Malaysia, and Thailand. Though traveling independently was allowed later, joining a group was for a long time the only option for someone who wished to go overseas. Even today, the language barrier, the difficulty of applying for a foreign visa, and the higher cost of going solo often discourage Chinese tourists from organizing their own trips. On top of that, the travel agencies didn't charge customers extra for sightseeing; they baked it into the price of the cruise ticket customers bought. That matched Chinese tourists' perception of how a cruise should work: a ticket should cover everything. The arrangement looked like a bad deal for travel agencies, but they made their money on the back end: They'd receive commissions from stores for bringing in shoppers. NCL did receive fees from travel agencies but not enough to compensate for its lost revenue.

The Last Straw

With onboard revenue failing to meet expectations, NCL depended even more on ticket sales. Those, too, didn't turn out as planned. A cruise line's revenue consists of tickets and onboard spending, with a typical ratio of about 70% tickets to 30% onboard revenue. *Joy* was profitable its first year in China, largely thanks to ticket sales. But the unique approach to ticket distribution in China influenced those solid early results. In the West, over 50% of tourists book their tickets directly with cruise companies. In contrast, cruise lines in China sell over 85% of their rooms through travel agencies as full-ship or half-ship charters; the agencies commit to the charters, buy the needed number of tickets from the cruise line, and then sell the tickets to individuals or groups.

NCL had started to sell tickets one year before *Joy*'s arrival, and the big new ship gave travel agencies enough confidence to commit. Their orders supported those positive first-year numbers. Yet when the travel agencies started pitching to Chinese tourists, they found *Joy* to be a hard sell. "Overall the ticket selling wasn't good," said Zhao. NCL thought *Joy* should command the highest prices, but the market didn't agree. In the eyes of Chinese tourists, Royal Caribbean, not NCL, was the premium player and thus deserved a premium price. This perception was a result of Royal Caribbean's decade-long effort to build a strong brand in China. In addition, Royal Caribbean had created a special sales team, with several hundred reps, that was sent to the travel agencies to help sell tickets. They helped convince customers who showed an interest in NCL or any other cruise line that it was worth the extra money to travel with Royal Caribbean.

A surge in the supply of cruises exacerbated NCL's predicament. *Joy* was not the only ship that entered China in 2017. Carnival's *Majestic Princess* arrived too, landing in Shanghai that July. They joined Royal Caribbean's *Quantum of the Seas*, which had come two years prior, so the world's three dominant cruise lines were docking at the same port. Add in other ships, like Star Cruises' *SuperStar Virgo* and SkySea Cruise Line's *Golden Era*, and there could be seven big boats in Shanghai. Still more ships were moored in other Chinese ports, like Tianjin, Guangzhou, and Shenzhen. The law of supply and demand affects cruise lines, just as it does everything else: When the supply exceeds demand, companies can't charge what they want.

Because of the oversupply, NCL had to find a way distinguish itself, which was what *Joy*'s China-specific design was supposed to do. Recall that *Joy* had been tailored for the Chinese market. But paradoxically that didn't help with ticket selling—it may have even backfired. The Chinese-style trappings looked too familiar to those who saw cruising as an exotic Western-style experience. "If it's too Chinese, then it's hard to sell," Zhao said. Chinese tourists were more drawn to features that felt foreign, like the British-style afternoon tea on Carnival's *Majestic Princess*, where sweet pasties, cakes, and tea were served by the cruise staff wearing white gloves.

As a result, travel agencies couldn't fill the ship at the prices they expected and had to start discounting. When one of them lowered the prices, others followed. Zhao's company sold tickets at less than 2,000 RMB (around $303) during its worst time, way below the price paid to NCL. "The majority of us were operating at a loss," she said. Afterward, agencies sent reports of their losses to NCL and sought compensation. "I knew we already signed the contract, but we really had no choice." NCL, the cruise line that put "partners first," returned to the negotiation table and agreed to provide additional cabins at no cost. Yet for Zhao, that just added more supply, without addressing the underlying issues. "The hole just became larger and larger," she said.

Alaska Calling

As difficulties accumulated in China, NCL released a new ship in Alaska in April 2018. The *Bliss*, which cost $1 billion to build, became a hit and reported a record profit. "That was by far the most successful launch we've ever had," said Andy Stuart, NCL's president at the time. Within a few months, NCL decided to move *Joy* to Alaska. "It was one of our more complicated decisions—after all, we had designed *Joy* for the Chinese market—but the more we watched *Bliss* perform, the more we realized this was a big opportunity," Stuart said.[13]

NCL announced *Joy*'s departure and promised to send another ship, *Spirit*, as a replacement. In a statement released then, the company said its commitment to China endured. Yet it only took a few months for NCL to reverse course. *Spirit* never arrived. NCL had set sail for other seas, leaving China marooned.

In April 2019, after 19 months in China, *Joy* steamed across the Pacific, destination Alaska. Before that journey, NCL had spent $50 million on an overhaul. The Chinese elements were removed, retail space and casinos were downsized, bars were added, and the spa and gym were expanded. US tourists probably wouldn't ever sense its past life in China.

Applying the Framework

Norwegian Cruise Line operated for less than two years in China before quitting. The decisive factors in that failure were as follows:

- NCL was just one more cruise company navigating crowded waters, with insufficient alpha assets. Unlike Royal Caribbean, which spent years building a brand in China, NCL didn't have a brand advantage and couldn't command the premium prices that Royal Caribbean did. Nor could it compete with the market coverage of Carnival, which operated several ships in China—cruise ships, in effect, serve as their own massive billboards, and Carnival had more. NCL only had *Joy*, and its itineraries (short trips to Japan) resembled those of its competitors.
- NCL didn't commit to the Chinese market in the way that Royal Caribbean and Carnival had. *Joy* operated for only 19 months, a record short time for a foreign cruise company in China. Then again, as with Amazon, NCL's decision to focus on Alaska may have maximized shareholder value in the long term and, from that perspective, may be hard to fault.
- In formulating its strategy, NCL misperceived *which* Chinese consumers would be drawn to its cruises. *Joy*'s large shopping area and three casinos seemed designed to attract the nouveau riche, who jetted around the world to shop and gambled enthusiastically. In reality, NCL found itself serving the emerging Chinese middle class, people who could afford a nice vacation but were prudent with their funds.

Table 3.1: Summary of Success Factors for Norwegian Cruise Line

Factor		Explanation
Demand	▲	Strong and growing demand for cruising in China.
Access to market	▲	Unfettered access to the market, with several strong Western competitors already operating.
Advantage	▽	No significant alpha assets.
Commitment	▽▽▽	Invested in one ship and operated it for only 19 months, then abandoned China, possibly because of high opportunity costs.
Governance	▽	Followed the typical multinational's China branch model. Strategic decision-making mainly happened at the headquarters.
Leadership		Led by an American executive who came from the CEO's inner circle. Seemed to lack knowledge of Chinese consumers.
Strategy	▽	Market segmentation and NCL focus proved inaccurate. The luxury consumer did not materialize as expected.
Product	▽▽	Ironically, significant localization likely detracted from the desirable foreignness of cruising.
Agility		Not particularly agile, but this likely hampered only tactical sales and marketing efforts.
Luck		The emergence of Alaska as a promising alternative target of opportunity was unexpected.

Note: Upward-pointing triangles indicate a positive factor. Downward-pointing triangles indicate a negative factor. The number of triangles is our subjective assessment of the relative importance of the factor. We omit indicators for those factors that we do not believe were significant for this case.

They didn't want to get sloshed in the onboard bars. They preferred to drink during meals, and NCL (to its credit) wasn't willing to try to strong-arm them to do otherwise.

- NCL bet heavily on *Joy*'s China-centric design. But being different didn't equate, in Chinese consumers' eyes, with being better. From the phoenix artwork on the topsides of the ship to the teahouses and karaoke rooms, *Joy* had many Chinese characteristics. Yet "Western-ness" is an attribute that can be valuable to foreign companies. As Chinese consumers become richer, they want to experience new things, so in this particular market, adapting the product too much to local tastes was likely the wrong strategy.

These elements and other factors in the framework are noted in Table 3.1, along with our subjective assessment of the decisive factors.

In China, Amazon and NCL—both successes elsewhere—possessed few alpha assets. That, combined with their limited willingness to invest in the face of compelling alternatives, led them to quickly say "bon voyage" to China. Next we'll focus on Hyundai, a company that had substantial alpha assets and bet billions over more than a decade.

Chapter 4

Hyundai
What Got You Here Won't Get You There

"We won't leave China," said Hyuk Joon Lee, vice president of Hyundai Motor (China).[1] At his office in eastern Beijing, a large map of the country hangs on the wall, marked by pushpins, indicating Hyundai's footprint in the world's largest auto market. Hyundai was a latecomer to China, entering in 2002, when Volkswagen, General Motors, Toyota, and other international automakers were already entrenched. But it managed to increase its China sales to 1 million vehicles annually in only a decade—a goal that took Volkswagen over 20 years to realize. In doing so, it became the country's third-largest auto manufacturer and took a more than 10% market share. Meanwhile, Lee honed his Chinese well enough that he earned a master's in business and a doctorate from Chinese universities. Hyundai seemed destined to thrive in China, as it had in the United States, overcoming doubters and establishing itself quickly as a maker of quality cars. Then came 2017.

That was the year China sales plummeted by more than 30%, presaging a slump that dragged through 2018 and 2019. Hyundai's market share shrank back to the low single digits, and the company closed one of its five factories—its factory in Beijing—and laid off over 2,000 employees, or around 13% of its workforce. Another factory in the southwest city of Chongqing, which opened in 2017, was cut to 50% capacity. "We are operating at a loss," Lee said. "But for the Chinese market, if you leave, there's no chance to come back."

A Weak Brand Meets a Weak Partner

Overseas expansion for Hyundai, Korea's dominant carmaker, started in the 1980s. It ventured successfully into the United Kingdom, the United States, and India. Then it tiptoed into China in the mid-1990s. Due to the Chinese government's quotas, it could export only around 200 cars to the country each year. Recalling that period, what struck Lee was the car prices. "A 200,000 RMB car (around $23,529) would be sold at 800,000 RMB (around $94,117) in China," he said. Even after China joined the World Trade Organization (WTO) in late 2001, opened its auto industry, and reduced the tariff significantly, barriers remained. Foreign automakers had to apply for an entry and stipulate the numbers of cars they aimed to sell. Without approval from the government, the door remained closed. The Koreans soon realized that the auto industry was one the government intended to protect and was unlikely to open completely to imports. Their answer was to produce cars in China. Volkswagen had done that and had come to be perceived by Chinese consumers as one of their own brands.

Back then, entering China required a joint venture with one of the eight state-owned Chinese automakers that had been awarded licenses to produce passenger cars. The chairman of the Committee of the Chinese People's Political Consultative Conference at the time, Ruihuan Li, a native of Tianjin, introduced Hyundai to Tianjin First Automobile Works (Tianjin FAW). Tianjin FAW had partnered with Toyota to produce the Xiali, a popular compact sedan, which sold nearly 100,000 units in 1998, accounting for 20% of China's car sales that year.[2] But Tianjin FAW turned Hyundai down on account of the latter's lack of brand recognition in China.

Then Hongqi, FAW's luxury brand, approached Hyundai. The general manager had an engineering background and was interested in Hyundai's technology. After a year of discussions, that company, too, passed on working with Hyundai. Its executives also regarded Hyundai as an unknown among Chinese car buyers.

Finally, Beijing Automotive Industry Holding (BAIC), a once glamorous yet troubled manufacturer, came forward. BAIC had collaborated with American Motor Corporation (AMC) to form the first Sino-Western auto joint venture, Beijing Jeep, back in 1984. But it had lately struggled and was rumored to be seeking a partner to avoid being acquired. Hyundai seemed its salvation. In October 2001, Hyundai and BAIC started talks, and the following May they formed a 50–50 joint venture. A few months later, in October, the Chinese state council approved the deal, a process that, according to Lee, would've normally taken three years. The Beijing municipality fast-tracked it to help a local company, and Beijing Hyundai came to life.

The Rise of an Underdog

The venture wasn't one that won headlines or worried competitors. After all, it was a marriage of a weak Chinese automaker and a "no-name" Korean partner. Still, Hyundai came prepared. Prior to its entry, the company created a unit called the China Business Management Team to lead the expansion. Lee was part of that team, and its members saw great potential in the Chinese market, which was growing about 20% a year. That growth was likely to continue as Chinese consumers, with increased income, replaced government bodies as the main buyers of cars. A market as big as China's could offer opportunities even to a latecomer. Hyundai extensively researched its rivals, probing for weaknesses. It found Toyota had been selling locally manufactured cars to Chinese consumers for 30% or more above the prices of comparable models in Japan and the United States. Other foreign brands often brought outdated models to China. Volkswagen's Chinese Jetta was based on a version from the 1980s.

Hyundai would bet on price *and* design. "We decided to bring our latest models with reasonable prices to Chinese consumers," Lee said. In December 2002, the EF Sonata, a midsize sedan, rolled off the assembly line at the Beijing plant. The model had been Hyundai's best seller in Korea and was priced at about 200,000 RMB ($24,390 in China). Compared with models from Toyota or Honda, which often sold for over 250,000 RMB, the car looked appealing. "I was often asked why I picked the unknown Hyundai over Volkswagen or any other brand that had been in China long enough to win us over," recalled Ning Zhu, a software engineer who bought an EF Sonata in 2003 with help from his parents. "Its design and appearance were superior. A definitely head-turning car boosted a 20-something young man's ego. And the price was cheaper than other foreign brands."[3]

Hyundai ended up selling 53,000 cars that first year, exceeding its expectations. "We thought we would sell 20,000 units or 25,000 units maximum," said Lee.

The early success stemmed partly from replicating Hyundai's established supply chain in the new territory. The EF Sonata hit the market only two months after the government approved the joint venture. Behind this record-breaking "Hyundai speed"—a term coined by Chinese media to describe Hyundai's ability to slash the time to get things done—was a tightly managed supply network. When Hyundai entered China, it pulled its main Korean suppliers in too—all of them were affiliates of Hyundai Group. Hyundai Mobis was one. Mobis is the world's sixth-largest auto-parts manufacturer. Hyundai Motor's CEO and chairman owns 7% of the company's shares, while Kia Motors, of which Hyundai owns 33%, controls 17%. And Mobis, in turn, is the biggest shareholder of Hyundai Motor, owning 20%. This interlocking shareholding structure, known as keiretsu, is typical of Korean conglomerates, and it bound Hyundai and Mobis tightly together.

Mobis located its Chinese branch in Shunyi district of Beijing, where the Beijing Hyundai factory was. Mobis and other Korean suppliers provided 80% of the components for the joint venture's cars, which ensured the quality and speed in the initial stage. "It was risky to come to China with us, but we had them come anyway," Lee said. "I doubt if Volkswagen or any other automakers had such influence over their suppliers." In fact, Volkswagen did have difficulty persuading skeptical suppliers to follow it to China during the early days and had been forced to build up a supplier network in the country. So Hyundai's supply chain was a strength—at first. Later, it would become a source of friction between the joint venture partners.

Hyundai introduced a second compact car, the Elantra, by the end of 2003, and the next year it almost tripled overall sales, to 144,000 cars. In 2005, that number increased again, to 233,000. That same year, another opportunity presented itself.

"Guanxi" Counts

Hyundai had first made an international name for itself at the 1988 Seoul Olympics as the national sponsor. It wanted to replicate that success in China by winning the sponsorship at the 2008 Beijing Olympics. It ended up losing out to Volkswagen, but the planning around the games offered up another opportunity: Beijing was upgrading its taxicab fleet. Hyundai realized that this too might let it market itself at the world's largest sports event.

Beijing's taxi fleet was around 67,000 vehicles and included Tianjin FAW's Xiali, Volkswagen's Jetta and Santana, and Peugeot-Citroen's Fukang. The incumbents wanted to remain, and new contenders, including Hyundai and several Chinese automakers, aimed to displace them. The Beijing government would, in effect, pick the provider by how it wrote its taxi standards; only cars that met the standards could serve as cabs in Beijing. Hyundai won big. Its outlook draft, designed by professors from Tsinghua University, was approved almost as soon as the standard committee saw it, according to Lee. The detailed standards, which included the dimensions of the car, engine capacity, safety equipment, and emissions, seemed tailored to the Sonata. Hyundai ended up providing 70% of the taxicabs for Beijing and soon became well known in China.

The following years saw Hyundai surge. Except for a blip in 2007, sales climbed. In 2013, they broke 1 million units. Hyundai kept launching new models, some of which were designed for the Chinese market. The Mistra, for example, had the long hood, additional rear legroom, a digital instrument panel, and the higher quality of interior trim that Chinese buyers preferred. Hyundai became the third-largest automaker in China, behind Volkswagen and General Motors. During this period, competitors would disassemble Hyundai's cars to study how they were made. "Hyundai seized on the opportunity and acted aggressively," said Dongshu Cui, secretary general at the National Passenger Cars Association. "It was a smash hit in China—superior design, diverse models, and competitive pricing."[4]

Homegrown Rivals

But Hyundai's strong position was soon to be undercut in ways that wouldn't have seemed possible just a few years earlier. When Hyundai first exported its cars to China in the mid-1990s, Shufu Li, an owner of a motorcycle company in the eastern Zhejiang province, was dreaming of making vehicles of his own. After extensive research, including having his technicians disassemble a Mercedes-Benz piece by piece, he concluded making cars wasn't that hard. It was just "four wheels and two sofas," he quipped.[5] In 1997, Li and his engineers made (by hand) their first car, the Geely No. 1, a mashup of the appearance of a Mercedes-Benz and the interior of a Hongqi. Two years later, the first of the company's mass-produced Haoqing cars rolled off the assembly line, selling at 55,800 RMB (around $6,804), a price that shocked the auto industry. Li's company soon introduced a series of small cars, and, by 2004, sales had broken 100,000. Yet a trip to the Frankfurt Auto Show in 2005, where the Geely was viewed as cheap and poorly built, set Li on a new path: acquisition.

In 2006, Geely Automobile acquired a 23% stake of London cab maker Manganese Bronze. The two formed a joint venture in Shanghai to produce cars under the name Englon. Two years later, Geely bought an Australian transmission supplier named Drivetrain Systems International. Another two years on, in a move that surprised the auto industry worldwide, Geely bought Volvo from Ford, as the US automaker struggled to repair its balance sheet during the financial crisis. Few in the industry believed Geely could turn around Volvo, which was struggling under Ford. Li took a hands-off stance, letting the Swedes at Volvo run their own shop. "Volvo is Volvo. Geely is Geely," he said. He stepped in only when necessary—for example, when Volvo sought to design a car with features Chinese consumers would prefer. Volvo has since built three plants in China and one in the United States and expanded its research centers in Sweden. By 2015, Volvo was selling over 500,000 vehicles a year, the best record in its 89-year history.[6] Geely, for its part, gained access to Volvo's technology, especially in safety, and that helped turn the Chinese parent company into a more credible brand among auto buyers. "Before the acquisition, we didn't completely master the design, research and engineering of a car, nor did we completely understand the manufacturing process," said Li. "Now we have it all figured out."[7]

In 2016, Geely launched a new high-end brand, Lynk & Co, and the first car, Lynk & Co 01, received 6,000 preorders within 137 seconds, according to Geely's records. Meanwhile, Geely's sales kept mounting, hitting 1.5 million in 2018, and eating into Hyundai's share.

Geely wasn't the only Chinese carmaker that emerged to challenge Hyundai. Another privately owned carmaker, Great Wall Motor, joined the auto club too. Founded in 1984, Great Wall initially did only modifications and repairs. In 1990, Jianjun Wei took over the debt-ridden company and turned it into a pickup-truck manufacturer. Great Wall focused on the domestic market and correctly predicted that Chinese consumers, like those in the United States, would shift their taste from sedans to SUVs. In 2002, it rolled out the first Safe SUV, priced at 80,000 RMB, and sold 30,000 units. Safe ended up becoming the third-best-selling SUV that year. Hyundai didn't release its first Tucson SUV until three years later and at a much higher price—around 200,000 RMB per unit.

In 2013, Great Wall launched a separate SUV brand, Haval, and hired former BMW designer Pierre Leclercq as head of design. The brand since has become a leader in the category and has topped the best-selling list for several years. Haval has further raised the profile of SUVs, and it helped lift Great Wall to the million-seller club in 2016. "Local players now are almost as good as Beijing Hyundai and at least 20,000 RMB cheaper," said Robert Bao, a board member at BAIC.[8]

As China's homegrown brands squeezed Hyundai, its foreign peers made life even harder. Unlike in the early days, when an outdated model could thrive and yield high margins, China had grown into one of the most competitive markets for the auto industry. Global automakers had to introduce new models to maintain their positions, and prices had to fall. Geely's Li once explained the evolution as follows: "Santana was sold for over 200,000 RMB, and Xiali was priced over 100,000 RMB when steel, plastics and labor were cheap in China. Now the cost of making a car has become expensive, but cars are so cheap. Why? Competition, brought by companies like us."[9]

When Toyota, Honda, General Motors, and other foreign automakers lowered their prices, there was not much room left for Hyundai. Hyundai's premium cars, such as the Equus, aimed to compete with Toyota's Lexus but couldn't command the same premium because they lacked the high-end brand image. "Chinese consumers care about two things," said Hyundai's Lee, "design and brand." Hyundai hadn't been able to distinguish itself with either. Its pioneering designs had been matched by its Chinese rivals, and its brand had remained the weakest among foreign automakers. Middle-class Chinese buyers preferred Volkswagens, Buicks, and Toyotas, while those in the luxury segment wanted Audis, BMWs, and Mercedes-Benzes.

Marital Conflict

While dealing with the increasingly competitive market, conflicts with BAIC started to spark. Hyundai and BAIC had had a blissful honeymoon. BAIC orchestrated the joint venture's lightning setup— from negotiations to production in a year; its chairman, Heyi Xu, was also a Beijing municipal official. And BAIC had helped Beijing Hyundai win that sizable taxicab business. Beijing Hyundai's early success, in turn, saved BAIC from the embarrassment of the AMC failure. Only one year after being established, the joint venture's revenue reached 9 billion RMB and contributed 12% of the industrial output of Beijing.[10]

Yet that honeymoon didn't last. A key conflict that emerged was over suppliers. Beijing Hyundai initially adopted Hyundai's suppliers to expedite production and ensure quality. Mobis, Wia, and a few other Korean firms controlled the supply network. BAIC grew dissatisfied with the arrangement. Beijing Hyundai's deputy general manager, Honglu Li, at the time said: "It's risky to have main parts coming from a single supplier."[11] Another drawback, from BAIC's perspective, was cost. As a latecomer, Beijing Hyundai offered competitive prices to gain market share. But sourcing from Korean suppliers, which often charged more than their Chinese counterparts, squeezed margins. Li admitted that Beijing Hyundai's profit was lower than the industry average.[12] But given the interlocked shareholdings between Hyundai Motor and Hyundai Mobis, industry analysts suspected that Hyundai Motor maintained this arrangement to support Mobis and eventually benefit from Mobis's gain. William Xu, deputy director of strategic planning at Baoneng Motor, a Chinese automaker, formerly worked in Beijing Hyundai's purchasing department. He confirmed the suspicion: "When Hyundai came to China, 90% of the top 50 suppliers were Korean. Because of this, Hyundai was able to profit through the parts companies."[13]

Whether Hyundai Motor has benefited from Mobis's sales to the joint venture is debatable, but a conflict between BAIC and Mobis boiled over when BAIC rejected Hyundai's proposal to cut the prices of their vehicles amid a sales slump in 2007. BAIC cited the high sourcing costs. "Previous price-cutting was at the expense of our joint venture's interest," said Honglu Li. "This is equivalent to drinking poison to quench thirst."[14] BAIC insisted on maintaining prices unless sourcing costs fell. The spat lasted for a few months, and Hyundai eventually conceded. Korean suppliers ended up lowering their prices, but BAIC didn't get what it fought for either: a supplier network that included more Chinese firms.

Following that wrangle, BAIC tried a different tact. In August 2007, it teamed up with Beijing Industrial Development Investment Management Company to form an auto parts company, with 60%

and 40% shares, respectively. According to BAIC's plans, this outfit, named Hainachuan, would provide parts to BAIC's subsidiaries, including Beijing Hyundai, Beijing Benz (joint venture between BAIC and Mercedes-Benz), and BAIC's own brands, including Foton Motor and Beijing Jeep. But that didn't happen with Beijing Hyundai; to this day, it mostly retains its Korean-dominated supply chain. Only recently did it open the network to others. "It's really difficult for Chinese local suppliers to get into Beijing Hyundai's supply network," said Weigang Chen, chief technology officer at Hainachuan. The percentage of parts Hainachuan provides to Beijing Benz is much higher than it provides to Beijing Hyundai, and Hyundai's closed system makes it difficult to control the cost, Chen added. "It's not a competitive environment but more like a monopoly."[15]

Xu noted another argument for Hainachuan's inability to break through: BAIC's relatively weak research and development capability. "Mobis was deeply involved with Hyundai Motor even during its early stage of car development," he said. "Mobis controls the platform, and it's hard for Hainachuan to replace it." If BAIC wants to get Hainachuan more involved, BAIC must play a bigger role in Beijing Hyundai's car development, following the example of Shanghai Automotive Industry Corp (SAIC). SAIC developed a low-emission engine with its joint venture partner General Motors and jointly owns the intellectual property. As a result, SAIC's auto-parts company, Huayu, plays a significant role in that joint venture's supply network. "Apparently BAIC doesn't possess the similar R&D capability," Xu said.

BAIC's weakness in R&D also undermines its influence on the joint venture, impeding Beijing Hyundai's responses to changing market conditions. If SAIC senses any change in the market, it can prompt the needed response. SAIC and another of its joint venture partners, Volkswagen, have launched vehicles specifically for China, developed jointly. BAIC doesn't have that kind of sway at Hyundai. Yet by relying only on Hyundai for new model development, their venture misses market opportunities. An example is SUVs. Though Beijing Hyundai introduced the Tucson in China in 2005, it had been slow to diversify its offerings and mostly missed the golden era of SUVs. "Xi25 and Santa Fe came out kind of late," Xu said. "In fact, it's not that Hyundai is too slow. It's the Chinese market that moves too fast to catch."

The THAAD Crisis

Amid all these pressures, Beijing Hyundai faced a crisis. In March 2017, the United States deployed a missile defense system called THAAD (Terminal High Altitude Area Defense) in Seoul. Both the United States and Korea say the radar system is meant to protect South Korea from North Korea, but China strenuously objected to its deployment, arguing it could be used to spy on its territory. Anti-Korea protests erupted across China. Korean products were boycotted. Korean TV dramas and music were removed from broadcasts. Trips to Korea were canceled. Lotte Mart, a Korean retailer that had rented its land for THAAD's deployment, ended up closing its 112 Chinese stores.

Hyundai, too, suffered. Sales plummeted from 1.14 million units in 2016 to 780,000 in 2017 and 790,000 units in 2018. The number dropped again, to 716,000, in 2019. This was when Hyundai shut down one of its five factories in Beijing and laid off over 2,000 employees. "It was THAAD," said Lee, vice president at Beijing Hyundai. "But we no longer even talk about THAAD anymore. It's something we have no control over." That's true inasmuch as Beijing Hyundai couldn't have planned for an "unknown unknown" like this. But, on account of its inflexible supply chain, it also likely lacked the agility to respond quickly.

Other automakers' responses to big setbacks in China suggest that THAAD wasn't Hyundai's only problem. Consider the Japanese companies. In 2012, they faced much more widespread protests and boycotts over Japan's control of disputed islands in the East China Sea. Sales of Japanese vehicles plunged, and Toyota, Nissan, and Honda cut their production in China roughly by half.[16] Yet, by the end of 2013, they had all recovered, with Toyota and Honda even seeing record sales.[17]

What's more, seven months after the THAAD boycotts had started, the Chinese government softened its stance. China and Korea agreed to normalize their relations, and China lifted the ban on group tours to Korea. Yet Beijing Hyundai's performance didn't rebound. Since the crisis, Beijing Hyundai has frequently changed its management team. On the Hyundai side, a new general manager arrived in September 2017, only to be replaced within a year. On the BAIC side, the deputy general manager also changed twice in the same period. "During the period when Beijing Hyundai had strong leadership from both sides, its performance was way better than other periods," Bao said. "Beijing Hyundai probably sat on their success for too long. The same product positioning and lineup helped them achieve that big role in the initial stage. So they kept the same strategy for years."

Now Beijing Hyundai is trying to elevate its brand, improve its technology, and invest in alternative-energy vehicles. Will it be able to return to the million-unit club in the near future, or will it follow its country mate Samsung, the maker of mobile phones, and fade from the Chinese market? That remains to be seen.

Applying the Framework

Hyundai has been in China for almost two decades and has experienced two distinct eras: success, then struggles. Here are some of the key explanatory factors:

- When Hyundai entered China, it possessed alpha assets. Unlike other foreign automakers, such as Volkswagen, which had to devote enormous effort and time to building a supply network, Hyundai replicated its sturdy Korean supply chain. That ensured quality and speed. Hyundai also scaled up its manufacturing quickly. For a while, the joint venture was the third-largest automaker in China, after Volkswagen and GM. The venture's initial product, a best-selling model brought directly from Korea, outperformed competitors, thanks to superior design. Coupled with competitive pricing, it was an immediate hit among Chinese consumers. Though Hyundai didn't have a strong brand, those three alpha assets carried it through its early years and contributed to its initial success.

- Hyundai's governance structure—a 50–50 joint venture with a local company—is inevitably more complex and unwieldy than other foreign companies' China setups. Both parent firms contributed key managers, yet the disagreements between them never stopped. That slowed decision-making and the ability to respond to China's rapidly changing market. When the performance of the joint venture deteriorated, both parents meddled, leaving less autonomy for the local executives. An extreme example was the executive upheaval from 2016 through 2018, when Hyundai replaced its general manager twice and BAIC replaced its vice general manager twice.

- Strategically, by partnering with BAIC, Hyundai aimed to start with cost leadership. Then, as China's middle class swelled and Hyundai's brand became established, it planned to move upmarket. But that strategy was never fully realized. Hyundai stalled out, doing well initially but never elevating its brand. Chinese automakers soon matched Hyundai's design capabilities, yet did so while retaining a cost advantage. Hyundai's Korea-centric supply network inhibited lowering costs. Other foreign automakers responded by updating their models and cutting prices, further squeezing Hyundai. Hyundai also lagged behind Chinese consumers' demand for more and better SUVs.

- And then there was THAAD. You have to call that bad luck. A question to consider is whether Hyundai could've better endured that crisis, in the way the Japanese carmakers did theirs, if its China operations and its relationship with BAIC had been stronger.

Table 4.1: Summary of Success Factors for Hyundai

Factor	Era I	Era II	Explanation
Demand	▲▲	▲▲	Strong and growing demand in China for automobiles.
Access to market			Hyundai navigated the regulated market by partnering with Beijing Automotive.
Advantage	▲▲▲	▲	Initially Hyundai had strong alpha assets in the form of supply chain, production capability, scale economies, and product design. Eventually these waned.
Commitment	▲▲▲	▲▲▲	Hyundai displayed a strong commitment to China, investing $15.8 billion and building five factories. It chose to stay even amid the THAAD crisis.
Governance	▽	▽	Governance structure—a 50-50 joint venture with a local company—is inevitably complex and unwieldy.
Leadership			Executives provided by both partner organizations.
Strategy	▲▲	▽▽	Hyundai aimed to start with cost leadership and later move up market. The second part of this strategy was not realized.
Product		▽	Initially, the product was successful with the Chinese middle class, but Hyundai failed to invest in innovation to track changing tastes.
Agility			Joint venture structure resulted in sluggish decision-making.
Luck		▽▽▽	THAAD was very bad luck.

Note: Upward-pointing triangles indicate a positive factor. Downward-pointing triangles indicate a negative factor. The number of triangles is our subjective assessment of the relative importance of the factor. We omit indicators for those factors that we do not believe were significant for this case.

These elements and other factors in the framework are noted in Table 4.1, along with our subjective assessment of the decisive factors.

We now turn to the story of LinkedIn, a company that remains in China, yet has struggled to meet its early expectations.

Chapter 5

LinkedIn
A Résumé for Success?

O n July 31, 2019, Chitu officially died. After four years, LinkedIn shut down Chitu, its China-only app. The app was named after a war horse in a Chinese historical novel, *Romance of the Three Kingdoms*. The horse was capable of running 1,000 miles in a day and climbing mountains as though galloping across flat land.

But in choosing the app's namesake, LinkedIn seemed to have forgotten the end of Chitu's story: The horse dies.

Every one of the leading tech companies has had flops, from Facebook's Paper to Amazon's Spark and Google's Google+. But Chitu was different—not just a failed product but more a shattered dream. Before Chitu, plenty of Western internet firms had struggled and failed in China. That forced LinkedIn to think differently as it designed Chitu. Derek Shen, then LinkedIn's China head, envisioned a networking site so appealing to young Chinese professionals that it would eventually lead to a public stock offering for LinkedIn China.[1]

A New Model

Reid Hoffman, cofounder and chairman of LinkedIn, long had an interest in China. According to a current LinkedIn executive who was involved in the China expansion,[2] the company's designs on China started in 2012, and Hoffman conducted extensive research about the Chinese market. This executive spoke on the condition of anonymity. At the time, China's dominant social platform was Weibo, which resembles Twitter. WeChat, the now ubiquitous multipurpose app, had just recently been released, and its main function was messaging. The idea of a Chinese version of LinkedIn initially met with skepticism. But Hoffman and his executives were accustomed to that kind of reaction—nearly every time LinkedIn had expanded to a new country, they'd been told that what had worked in the United States wouldn't work locally. Every time, the naysayers had been wrong.

Hoffman and his executive team believed Chinese professionals would respond similarly. Though LinkedIn didn't have a China-specific online offering, it had already amassed a few million Chinese users, solid evidence of potential. So LinkedIn liked its odds when it officially arrived in China on January 1, 2014.

Back then, an internet company entering China had to have a local partner. LinkedIn had two options: a tech firm or a financial backer. Pairing with Chinese tech companies, like Baidu, Alibaba, or Tencent, had an obvious appeal. That would give LinkedIn rich industry distribution. But the downside was equally obvious: once the local firm learned your business—and your users—it could "cut you off," said the current LinkedIn executive. A financial partner, in contrast, could help navigate the Chinese business and regulatory environments but wouldn't take too much control. LinkedIn opted for the latter, giving up a small part of its local operation to two well-known Chinese venture capital firms: Sequoia China and China Broadband Capital. Sequoia China is run by Neil Shen, who had frequently appeared atop *Forbes* magazine's Midas List and invested in almost half of China's internet companies. China Broadband Capital was founded by Edward Tian, who set up China's first internet company, Asiainfo, in 1993 and then headed China Netcom, a state-owned telecommunications company. Both men brought connections. It didn't take LinkedIn too long to obtain an internet content provider license, a prerequisite for operating in China; that had taken Google a few years. LinkedIn also landed its China president, Derek Shen, through Neil Shen's network. (The two Shens are not related.) In an interview with Bloomberg TV, LinkedIn's CEO, Jeff Weiner, lavished praise on Derek in front of an audience of millions: "Our China president . . . is an entrepreneur at heart, an engineer by training."[3]

Derek had grown up in China and been educated in the United States. After earning a master's in computer science from the University of California at Los Angeles, he worked for Verizon, Yahoo, and Google. He then built Nuomi, a Chinese start-up later acquired by Baidu, China's leading internet search company. He was one of the few candidates who met LinkedIn's criteria: He had a tech background and corporate and start-up experience and understood both China and the United States.

Weiner had promised him autonomy to entice him to take the job. He even changed LinkedIn's structure to have Shen report directly to him. "Historically some companies stumbled or experienced challenges, and in part that's coming from having your head of China report to head of international, who may or may not report to the CEO," said Weiner.[4] Weiner also announced that LinkedIn China would do its own development, meaning the China product would be adapted to local conditions beyond just language. That level of localization was an exception for LinkedIn. LinkedIn China had its own board, consisting of five members: Hoffman, Weiner, Neil Shen, Tian, and Derek Shen. The China team was offered stock options, a reward system similar to that of other start-ups in China. The idea was to run LinkedIn China as a start-up so that it could better compete in the hurly-burly of the Chinese market. In LinkedIn's view, China was too competitive for edicts from far away—too many constraints from headquarters would hasten failure. Plus, flexibility would enable the local team to find its own way.

Blending into the Chinese Internet Ecosystem

The original LinkedIn had started out in 2002 relying on email for user acquisition. Email, of course, was a key business tool in the United States. In the early days, Hoffman personally emailed his contacts in and around Silicon Valley, inviting them to join his newly created venture. Search engine optimization also helped. In the

United States, when you search online for someone's name, that person's LinkedIn profile often pops up. Yet neither of those approaches seemed suited for China. Email had never dominated there in the way it has in the United States. Chinese people often opted for phone calls or WeChat as their main means of communication, and Baidu, the Chinese-language search engine, was unlikely to return a LinkedIn profile.

The LinkedIn China team accepted these realities. They struck a deal with WeChat, linking WeChat to LinkedIn accounts. When Hoffman had visited China in 2012, WeChat, owned by Tencent, had just launched. Two years later, it replaced Weibo as China's favorite social app, hosting around 400 million monthly users. In addition to messaging, people used it for video calls, status updates, mobile payments, and ride hailing. It was the backbone of China's social internet.

Yet WeChat wasn't a natural partner for a professional networking site. Its user profiles were scanty, even fictional. A user name wasn't necessarily that person's real name, and a profile picture typically bore little resemblance to the actual person behind the smartphone or keyboard. It could be a dog or cat or anything else. One user called himself "Franklin" and put a picture of the US Founding Father Benjamin Franklin next to his name. So LinkedIn did bring a benefit to WeChat: It provided detailed user information, which had value in the business context. "Many users found us through WeChat," said Linus Chung, former head of corporate development at LinkedIn China.[5] The partnership significantly boosted LinkedIn's exposure in China.

Another LinkedIn enticement was its relationship with Sesame Credit, a credit-scoring system developed by an affiliate of Alibaba and embedded in its popular payment tool, Alipay. Sesame Credit offered perks to people with good credit, such as easier access to loans, waivers on rental deposits, and a simplified visa application for overseas travel. Credit scores were calculated based on several factors, including transactions on Alibaba's sites, social media interactions, and payment history via Alipay. LinkedIn became one of the variables—people with LinkedIn profiles would be awarded higher scores, another reason to sign up.

The relationships with WeChat and Sesame Credit worked so well that Mark Feng, former product lead at LinkedIn China, even devised a new definition of localization: "adjusting your product structure to make it compatible to that of Chinese tech giants, who shaped the internet landscape and user behavior."[6] Feng was recruited in California and sent to Beijing, where he and his team localized LinkedIn to cater to Chinese users' preferences. They added new features, such as the ability to find people nearby and Chinese news recommendations. But none of these brought returns as great as the integrations with WeChat and Sesame Credit.

Another way in which LinkedIn China departed from the parent company's orthodoxy was its willingness to operate off-line, using ads and events to increase awareness and adoption, a method widely used by Chinese internet companies. LinkedIn did an ad campaign in Beijing's and Shanghai's teeming subway stations; Beijing and Shanghai have the busiest subway systems in the world, each with more than 9 million riders a day. In the ads, Reid Hoffman and three Chinese celebrity endorsers—Olympic gymnast Ning Li, English teacher turned investor Xiaoping Xu, and pop singer Haiquan Hu— invited Chinese commuters to go on LinkedIn. The significance of Hoffman's embrace of traditional advertising wasn't lost on Derek Shen. He recalled proposing ad campaigns to Google, his previous employer, and being rejected by headquarters executives who found the idea bizarre: "Why would an internet company run off-line ads?" But LinkedIn, as he'd been promised, was willing to adapt to what the local market demanded and what the local team judged prudent. "We got a simple answer: You decide!" said Derek Shen.[7]

LinkedIn also organized hundreds of meetups, inviting Chinese professionals to meet with high-profile career "mentors," including Hoffman, Neil Shen, PayPal cofounder Peter Thiel, and Kaifu Lee, an investor and former president of Google China. Those efforts paid off, as user numbers climbed. They jumped from 4 million in the beginning of 2014 to 9 million by the middle of 2015.

"Constraints" from Headquarters

Despite the progress, Derek Shen, even with his autonomy, found himself constrained. He wanted to tweak LinkedIn's registration to make it more China-centric. China is a mobile-first market—people access the internet via their mobile phones more so than in any other country, and when they register for a new app, they're often asked for a cell phone number. Yet LinkedIn's app was based on email. The company assumed everyone had an email account. But in China, email users accounted for only about one-third of total internet users. But adding a mobile registration had to be done by engineers in California, on LinkedIn's global platform, where a minor change would impact all regions where LinkedIn operated. "Any product modification for the Chinese market on our global platform was extremely difficult and slow," said Robin Zhang,[8] the former chief of staff to LinkedIn China's president. As a result, over a year after LinkedIn entered China, registration via cell phone was still not available. That bothered Derek Shen. He complained to Neil Shen that this kind of change would've taken a Chinese start-up a couple of weeks.[9]

The same sort of frustration arose with the integration with Alipay. Again, the headquarters had to be involved, and LinkedIn China had to wait its turn unless the request was escalated to a special case or Derek Shen found an advocate at the headquarters who believed in the project. Local autonomy meant freedom to fast-track whatever the team wanted *in China*, but at a corporation with LinkedIn's size, you still needed relationships in the home office when you wanted something done there. Weiner had promised that when the China team needed the help of functional areas not located in China, he'd impart the needed sense of urgency. In reality, the message didn't always get through. "All those fundamental things sound great on PowerPoint slides when you educate executives in the US about China, and everybody sort of nods his head," said Chung. "But when you get to how you operate on the daily basis, it's really difficult."

And that wasn't the only disagreement with headquarters. Silicon Valley companies have long held they need not pay for growth because a good product sells itself. Chinese tech companies, in contrast, tend to spend a lot for product adoption. Advertising and other off-line promotions are common. As a result, though the initial ad campaign was approved by headquarters, the China team was rebuffed when it wanted to double down. "An American executive, who's used to ROI and believes that our product should be good enough to have people come flocking, wouldn't be convinced," Chung said. He believed both the home office's bias about not paying for growth and the local team's failure to build a convincing case contributed to the impasse. "Our cases were usually based on what everybody else did, not why we needed to do it. And we had a limited budget and short leash with the headquarters."

Executives in California grew disenchanted with the meetups too. They started to question their value, in particular Hoffman's participation. The events seemed to result in improvement only in vanity metrics: The number of attendees didn't equate to the same number of new LinkedIn users. Attendees were drawn to the well-known speakers but not to LinkedIn. Chung faulted the execution. "Some events didn't even require attendees to sign up on LinkedIn. Instead they were asked to register with their cell phones or just follow LinkedIn on WeChat," he said.

The Birth of Chitu

In March 2015, Derek Shen flew to California and made a bold proposal: He wanted to launch a separate professional networking app.[10] Weiner's first reaction, according to Shen, was: "Are you crazy?" Shen had anticipated that and had come with answers. LinkedIn, he pointed out, was born in the PC era, and its email-centered design didn't fit the mobile-first Chinese market. The LinkedIn brand likewise appealed only to the few Chinese who spoke English and had overseas experience or worked at multinationals. What's more, integrating with the standardized global product had prevented

LinkedIn China from operating like a local start-up—something the China board, which of course included Weiner and Hoffman, had wanted from the beginning.

Shen's proposal also drew on the classic example of QQ and WeChat. When Tencent spotted the shift from PC to the mobile internet, it didn't convert QQ, its web-based messaging service, into a mobile app. It started from scratch. That was how WeChat came to life.

Weiner eventually agreed. Shen recalled him saying, "I see the risks of doing this, but I also see the risks of not doing this."[11] According to the current LinkedIn executive, this decision was based on the original thesis: the idea of fully empowering the local team.

Shen was delighted; he finally got the autonomy he'd been promised. He and his China team were given complete control over the new product's development and operation, without intervention from headquarters. Shen had his own theory of how a multinational firm could succeed in China. He believed it had to meet three criteria. It had to be led by an entrepreneur, not a corporate executive. It had to have autonomy. And its product or service had to be tailored to China and not just be a modification of a standardized global product. With Weiner's decision, he'd checked all three boxes.

He immediately hired an engineering team for the app, and its members worked tirelessly, including staying at a hotel for a month without weekends off. Three months later, in June 2015, the new app was launched. It was of course named Chitu, and the hope was that it would be speedily adopted by non-English-speaking young professionals. LinkedIn, meanwhile, would remain the high-end brand in China, targeting more mature users with international backgrounds.

Chitu Falters

Chitu solved the long-standing mobile registration problem, and it included QR-code scanning for adding new connections. Other new features were "knowledge sharing," where an array of industry experts talked about career-related topics via voice broadcasting, and announcements of off-line events. Beyond that, there was not much difference between Chitu and LinkedIn. Even the China team sensed that.

"We just realized that Chitu bore too many resemblances to LinkedIn," said Zhang. "The longer we ran Chitu, the more we felt that way."

Chitu and LinkedIn didn't turn out to complement each other in the way that WeChat and QQ had. WeChat had enough differentiated features to drive QQ users to WeChat, and people ended up using both products. But Chitu users and LinkedIn users were separate groups, with almost no overlap. That was an irony for a social networking company: The app created a divide, not a connection.

In addition, with Chitu divorced from LinkedIn's global platform, it lost its parent's strengths. By the time LinkedIn entered China, there were about a dozen companies targeting professional online networking. Among them were Tianji, the Chinese branch of a French network, Viadeo; Ushi, a creation of Canadian entrepreneur Dominic Penaloza; and such Chinese firms as Maimai, Dajie, Renhe, Weaklink, and Jingwei. What had set LinkedIn apart was its global network, something no one else had. Yet Chitu, by cutting ties with its parent, lost that.

But the implacable competitor Chitu faced wasn't any of the professional networking competitors. It was WeChat. Unlike in the West, where people post to Facebook for family and friends and LinkedIn for work, the Chinese don't separate their personal and professional networks. Everything's posted on WeChat. You can see pictures from someone's family vacation in Tokyo on Tuesday and her shots of a customer event in Shanghai on Friday. Though WeChat began as an offshoot of a social network, it had broadened into an "omni app," providing all sorts of useful functions, such as free video/audio calls, file transferring, and group chat. As a result, many professionals had come to depend on it in their jobs. In business settings, it had become common in China to just add each other's WeChat information instead of exchanging business cards. Once people were connected on WeChat, there was little reason for them to move to another platform.

One feature WeChat lacked but Chitu had was a pool of professional profiles, which let Chitu users search for various skills, characteristics, and affiliations. But that sort of functionality appealed less to professionals than to headhunters. Chitu also touted expanding one's network and looking for opportunities via "weak ties." But that idea sounded foreign in China; it's not how the Chinese interact. China remains a society where people meet—and build guanxi— mainly through acquaintances. Online professional networking is a hard sell in such a place.

The Chitu team sensed that. So they decided to bet on knowledge sharing, hoping this would set Chitu apart. "We had run 1,000 sessions of knowledge sharing within one year," said Zhang. They even changed Chitu's slogan from "the app that understands China's professional networking the most" to "the app that shares deep and interesting career knowledge." That didn't work either.

Chitu was not alone in its struggles. Both Viadeo and Ushi exited China in 2015, even though Viadeo had accumulated 15 million users. Other platforms had repositioned themselves toward job searches. An exception was Maimai. Launched in 2013, it offered similar services to the others but gained traction through its anonymous chat feature, where users shared industry and office gossip under pseudonyms. Corruption allegations against Ofo, China's once-hot bike-sharing start-up, first broke on Maimai. That generated national headlines, which brought in many new users. Maimai secured $200 million in a round of financing in 2018 and announced plans to go public in 2019. During its fund-raising period, Chinese authorities asked Maimai to close its anonymous posting section, out of concern that it spread false rumors, violated privacy, and raised other legal issues. Maimai complied. It was still growing, yet throughout 2019 there was no news on its initial public offering (IPO). Rumors circulated that it had lost its appeal as a result of removing anonymous chatting. "Would Maimai be a big player like LinkedIn in the US? I don't know," said Neil Shen. "LinkedIn is a very successful model in the US. But if you look at China, that model never worked."[12]

Chitu or LinkedIn?

Chitu's external struggles were mirrored by conflicts within LinkedIn China. Since Chitu's launch in 2015, the China team had given it priority and let LinkedIn languish. When the idea of starting a new app was broached, some of the team members had raised concerns about whether it was practical to run two products simultaneously. They were being proved right.

"As soon as we got that engineering team signed off and the new product was running, people just started ignoring LinkedIn," Chung said. According to Chung, resources assigned to LinkedIn were diverted to Chitu. For instance, after Sesame Credit drove growth for LinkedIn, the team started pushing a partnership with Chitu. "That was equivalent of starving potential growth for your global network."

Without continued attention and investment, LinkedIn lost whatever appeal it had. It was still attracting new users, but their engagement rate remained low. Many Chinese professionals would create a profile and never return. A former LinkedIn marketing employee told the *New York Times* that LinkedIn's Australia network had far few users but was much more active.[13]

Seeing the slippage, executives in California ended their hands-off policy. They sent staffers to China to investigate. In June 2017, after two years of running Chitu, Derek Shen stepped down. In his farewell letter, posted on LinkedIn,[14] he said: "It is difficult for multinational internet companies to operate in China. It's even more difficult to build a new business model within a well-established multinational firm. But we fulfilled our mission." He summarized LinkedIn China's achievement thusly: 32 million users and tens of millions dollars in revenue. He didn't mention Chitu.

After his departure, the company started to scale back from Chitu and refocus on LinkedIn. For the next 10 months, an interim president oversaw the operation, until Jian Lu was hired to take over. Like Derek Shen, Lu also had a tech background, experience in both big corporations and start-ups, and ties to both China and the United States. Despite those similarities, Lu's line of reporting looked much different. The privilege of reporting directly to the global CEO Weiner was gone. Lu answered to the global head of engineering. In May 2019, Lu announced a new strategy for LinkedIn China, shifting its focus from professional networking to career development. The site would now stress its career guides, salary insights, and workplace Q&As. Two months later, Chitu went off-line.

Apart from the failed Chitu experiment, LinkedIn is still held up as a model of how a multinational can succeed in China. For LinkedIn, success meant—and continues to mean—fulfilling its mission by connecting 140 million Chinese professionals with each other and with the rest of LinkedIn's worldwide network of nearly 700 million people. That's why it's still there. What it hasn't done is to establish itself as a dominant site. "Nobody expects to make money any time soon in China," said the current LinkedIn executive. "We managed to beat everyone by still being there."

Applying the Framework

The LinkedIn story isn't done. While we admire LinkedIn's continued commitment, its initial expectations clearly were not realized. Here are some of the key explanatory factors:

- Demand for online professional networking in China is not
  yet evident. Many have tried and failed to be the "LinkedIn
  of China." If the job to be done is to enable and encourage
  online professional networking, as in other markets,
  then demand has not yet emerged in the Chinese market.
  However, if the job to be done is to allow professionals
  to realize their career goals, then a lot of demand exists.
  From the outset, LinkedIn had reason to believe that the
  job it performed in the rest of the world existed in China.

Hoffman and other members of the executive team had often heard the refrain "it doesn't work that way here," and they'd shown that again and again to be wrong. In many other global markets, preferences for LinkedIn developed as its benefits became clear. As coauthors we still regularly debate the question of whether demand for online professional networking will develop in China, but to date this uncertainty has not been resolved.

- In its home country, LinkedIn's alpha assets include brand, product, scale, and its massive network. Yet in China, most of those were *not* alpha assets. Most Chinese professionals had never heard of the brand, and the product resembled competitors' offerings. Upon its entry, LinkedIn did have 4 million users in China, but that was a tiny fraction of the country's 140 million professionals. LinkedIn's only real remaining advantage was its global network, which none of its competitors possessed. Once a Chinese professional joined, that person had access to professionals from around the world. Some may argue that a global network would appeal only to Chinese who wanted to connect to people outside China. But what if a group of Chinese who *didn't* have an interest in a global network wanted to connect with those Chinese who *did*? And what if more people followed this lead? The network effect could be powerful, though the question is how to leverage it to LinkedIn's benefit in a country where culture and preferences impact the way people interact with each other on an online platform. This remains today a credible thesis for how LinkedIn could still thrive in China.

- LinkedIn's local team was led by a US-educated Chinese entrepreneur with Western corporate experience; he seemed ideal for the job. Yet he wasn't able to secure the resources and support his unit needed, despite endorsements from both Hoffman and Weiner. He ended up, in effect, cutting ties with the parent and starting a new platform.

Table 5.1: Summary of Success Factors for LinkedIn

Factor		Explanation
Demand	▽	Demand for online professional networking not yet proved.
Access to market		To avoid repeating mistakes made by other foreign companies, LinkedIn developed a new operational model by forming a joint venture with Chinese venture capital firms. In doing so, it acquired the legal and regulatory expertise it needed while avoiding the peril of partnering with a future rival.
Advantage	▽	Brand and customer network are clear alpha assets in most of LinkedIn's markets. Brand offered no significant advantage in China, and LinkedIn's strategy did not focus on the value of its global customer network.
Commitment	▲	LinkedIn demonstrated a strong commitment to China, born of Hoffman's vision and the company's values. The company said it didn't expect immediate return. Its commitment stemmed from its mission of connecting the world's professionals, including those in China.
Governance		The company's governance structure granted a lot of autonomy to the China unit. Recall Derek Shen's direct reporting line to the global CEO and the stock options granted to the China team.
Leadership	▽	Derek Shen enjoyed support from company leadership but was unable to marshal resources from headquarters at an operational level. He was suited to lead an autonomous effort to build Chitu, but that goal was probably misguided.
Strategy	▽▽▽	LinkedIn's strategy was to build a completely local product, Chitu. In retrospect, this strategy failed to exploit LinkedIn's alpha assets and gave it no particular advantage over more nimble start-ups.
Product	▽	LinkedIn and all of its competitors have yet to find product-market fit.
Agility	▽▽	Initial governance structure was designed to accelerate decision-making and let LinkedIn China run like a start-up. Now, LinkedIn China operates more like the branch of a multinational, and thus it appears to have lost some of its agility.
Luck		No particularly decisive positive or negative exogenous events.

Note: Upward-pointing triangles indicate a positive factor. Downward-pointing triangles indicate a negative factor. The number of triangles is our subjective assessment of the relative importance of the factor. We omit indicators for those factors that we do not believe were significant for this case.

That reduced interference from headquarters and provided autonomy but ended up looking like a mistake when the app wasn't widely adopted. The LinkedIn China experience highlights the central tension of autonomy. A China unit must be granted the agility to compete in China. But if it doesn't leverage its parent's assets, it has no particular advantage, relative to aggressive local rivals.

- LinkedIn's strategy quickly shifted to complete localization by building Chitu. That only put it in the same position as its competitors, especially when facing WeChat, China's dominant social media tool, widely used for both business and personal life. Without its central alpha asset, LinkedIn had no strength to play. In retrospect, the strategy of a separate product was probably a key misstep.

- To borrow a marketing phrase, LinkedIn struggled to find "product-market" fit. The company's worldwide positioning as a professional networking platform didn't work well in China (though it may still). Chitu represented a repudiation of that approach. Even today, LinkedIn has only partially realized product-market fit. Mind you, the same could be said about competitors. The winning approach to professional networking in China remains to be seen.

These elements and other factors in the framework are noted in Table 5.1, along with our subjective assessment of the decisive factors.

LinkedIn completes our four cases of companies that either exited China or didn't meet their expectations there. Starting with the next chapter, we'll see how another four companies used their alpha assets and managerial strengths—with the help, of course, of some good fortune—to win in China.

Chapter 6

Sequoia Capital
Weaving Filaments Across Borders

It was a Saturday in June 2019, and Doug Leone, managing partner of Sequoia Capital, was waiting for 50 Chinese guests to arrive at his house in Los Altos Hills, California, one of the towns that make up Silicon Valley. Over the past decade, he'd traveled to China dozens of times, and now over half of his venture capital firm's assets under management were invested there. China mattered mightily to Sequoia's continued fortunes, and so did Leone's Chinese guests. Among them was Neil Shen (whom we first met in chapter 5 with LinkedIn), a colleague who ran Sequoia China. In both 2018 and 2019, Shen had topped the *Forbes* Midas List, a ranking of the world's 100 top venture capitalists. The companies he'd backed had included ecommerce giants Alibaba and JD.com, group-buying website Meituan-Dianping, and ride-hailing company Didi Chuxing, which eventually drove Uber off China's streets. The returns to Sequoia's limited partners had been substantial. Out of over 500 companies Sequoia China had invested in since its 2005 inception, 53 were valued at more than $1 billion each.

Sequoia was not the first foreign venture capital firm to enter China. IDG Capital had arrived in the 1990s, and New Enterprise Associates opened its Chinese operation in 2003. Other well-known firms had followed Sequoia, including, in 2007, Kleiner Perkins, its neighbor on famed Sand Hill Road in Menlo Park, California, another Silicon Valley community. Yet Sequoia's success amid this crowd had exceeded even Leone's dreams. "It's way better than we ever imagined," he said.[1]

He recalled how it began in 2004, five years after Sequoia's first overseas venture in Israel. Back then, he'd written a one-page memo that listed the reasons to expand to the Far East. It started like this: "I'm not sure whether it's for defense or offense." On the defensive side, he reasoned, many of the most talented entrepreneurs in the United States were immigrants, and Chinese start-ups were flocking to the United States for IPOs. Sequoia needed to position itself to be the preferred venture capital firm of Chinese-born entrepreneurs. Otherwise, their start-ups would end up in rival firms' portfolios. On the offensive side, Sequoia aimed to be the largest outside shareholder in the most valuable companies in the world. These kinds of companies were increasingly coming from fast-growing economies in the developing world, and China dwarfed nearly all of them. "Back then, we didn't go to Europe, because it was large but was not growing fast," Leone said. "We didn't go to Vietnam, because it was growing fast but wasn't very big. That took us right away to China." Plus, several of Sequoia's partners were born cosmopolitans—Leone was originally from Italy, and his partner Michael Moritz from Britain.

When Leone and Moritz started traveling to China, they were aware of how other firms were approaching the country—these outfits typically shuttled their partners back and forth from the United States. Sequoia set out to find a local partner, ideally someone who had spent time in the United States, had contacts in China, and had experience as an entrepreneur. They took 10 trips to China and took dozens of meetings, trying to identify someone who fit their ideal.

None of their efforts yielded the person they sought. Then, after returning home, a Chinese founder of Billpoint, a Sequoia investment and the predecessor to PayPal, introduced them to Shen. Leone, Moritz, and Shen met at a hotel in San Francisco. Sequoia's search ended there.

Within 30 days they had a handshake deal, and, shortly after, Moritz crafted a private placement memorandum for Sequoia China and handed it to Shen. Shen remembers being impressed by the trust, confidence, and agility shown by Sequoia.[2] The fact that the deal was cut quickly also reflected Shen's strengths. Growing up in Shanghai, he'd excelled at math. After graduating from Yale School of Management in 1992, he'd started his career as an investment banker in New York and Hong Kong. When the first internet wave reached mainland China in 1999, Shen left banking and cofounded Ctrip, a travel company, and later Home Inn, a budget hotel chain. Both went public on the Nasdaq. Yet Leone also appreciated Shen's acumen when it came to investing in other people's ventures. He'd displayed that with a bet on Focus Media, an investment made while he was running Ctrip. "He aligned himself with winners," Leone said.

What appealed to Shen was Sequoia's history of backing many of Silicon Valley's legendary companies, including Apple, Google, and PayPal. That would matter to Chinese entrepreneurs. The message was plain, Shen said: Sequoia "would help you to succeed." Sequoia China's initial fund-raising went well, with $160 million collected within three months, almost all from the universities, pension funds, and other institutions that had participated in Sequoia's US investment funds. (A venture capital firm typically raises money from institutional investors for a series of so-called funds, the money from which is invested in promising companies. The venture firm is the general partner of each of the funds, and the institutional investors are limited partners.)

Entrepreneurship Takes Off in China

The word "entrepreneurship" didn't really resonate in China until the new economy, powered by the internet, emerged in the late 1990s. Suddenly, starting a business no longer required a heavy up-front investment. With just a bank of computers, an ambitious Chinese technologist could create ventures similar to those emerging abroad. Shen's first start-up, Ctrip, had been inspired by Expedia. And that helped shape his pitch to Chinese entrepreneurs: "There's a chance that you, too, can do that in China."

To understand Chinese entrepreneurs' admiration of Silicon Valley's famed entrepreneurs, a few stories may help. Jun Lei, the billionaire founder of smartphone-maker Xiaomi, aimed to emulate Steve Jobs and build a company that could change the world.[3] When he introduced new products on stage, he would wear Jobs's signature black tee and blue jeans, earning him the nickname "Leibs"—one he was happy to claim. Likewise, Xing Wang, Meituan-Dianping's cofounder, had stumbled, with failed clones of Facebook and Twitter, before eventually taking Meituan-Dianping public. When Meituan-Dianping was listed on the Hong Kong Stock Exchange, he didn't thank Facebook's Mark Zuckerberg or Twitter's Jack Dorsey. He thanked Jobs. "Without the iPhone and mobile internet, everything we do today wouldn't have been possible," he said.[4]

Elon Musk, who seems to strive to be larger than life, had similarly amassed a fan base in China. His biography, *Elon Musk: Tesla, SpaceX, and the Quest for a Fantastic Future*, was translated into Chinese with an exuberant title—*Elon Musk: Iron Man's Adventurous Life*—and was marketed as an entrepreneur's must-read. At one point, Xiaopeng He, cofounder of Xiaopeng Motors, an electric vehicle company, faced a lawsuit from Tesla. Yet that didn't diminish his ardor for Musk. "To change China, we need crazy guys like him," he said.[5]

Imagine the venture firm that had partnered with Jobs and Musk reaching out to a Chinese entrepreneur. What would the likely response be? In 2005, Xing Wang fielded just such an inquiry. His initial response—"Sequoia? Never heard of it"[6]—reflected the firm's low profile in China at the time. Sequoia had just opened its China office and was using its translated Chinese name, Hongshan. When Wang realized that Hongshan was the prestigious venture investor from Silicon Valley, he rushed over that same afternoon to its Beijing office. A few years later, Ya Shen, the founder of the ecommerce company Vipshop, received a message from Sequoia via his company's customer service desk (yes, Sequoia still cold calls entrepreneurs it's interested in). He promptly returned the call.

Seeking an Edge

A storied name is not the only alpha asset Sequoia brought to China. Its investment team came with strong hands-on knowledge of how to run growing companies with big dreams. Sequoia's preference for "operators"—that is, partners with operating experience—dates back to the firm's beginnings. The late Don Valentine, the founder, spent over 10 years at Fairchild Semiconductor and National Semiconductor before starting the firm in 1972. His knowledge of microprocessors rivaled that of almost anyone in investment circles back in the 1970s. In a personal account, he wrote: "For a long time on the West Coast, I had a tremendously unfair advantage, because none of the other people understood much about technology."[7]

Leone followed a similar path, coming to Sequoia via Sun Microsystems and Hewlett-Packard. After he and Michael Moritz took over, they kept inviting seasoned tech executives and entrepreneurs to join the team. Bryan Schreier arrived from Google, Alfred Lin from Zappos, and Omar Hamoui from AdMob. Shen continued that tradition in China. In 2005, he hired Kui Zhou, an investor from Legend Capital. But before that, Shen said, "he was running a factory in Guangdong." Shen insists on that approach in recruiting staffers for his office: "An important component of making a good investor is industry knowledge."

That comports with Valentine's view. He eschewed financial engineering and believed the venture business was about building companies. Valentine's deep knowledge of microprocessors and their applications led to Sequoia's investment in Apple. "Knowing about microprocessors made the evolution of the PC obvious," he said.[8] Then, based on its investment in the PC industry, Sequoia developed an understanding of the internet and identified the potential of the networking industry, which directed the firm to Cisco.

Shen and his team have operated similarly. Sequoia China was one of the first venture firms to bet on ecommerce—today a $1.9 trillion market. That stemmed from Shen's experiences at Ctrip, his online booking site. Shen saw investing in ecommerce as a simple progression from where he'd started. Thus Sequoia China has also partnered with Alibaba, JD.com, PDD, Vipshop, and a variety of other Chinese ecommerce companies.

The rise of ecommerce has changed Chinese consumers' shopping, just as it's changed shopping in the developed world. Online purchases started simple, with people buying relatively inexpensive, easy-to-evaluate items, like apparel and cosmetics, but purchases have moved to more complex transactions, like prepared food. That shift created the online-to-off-line (O2O) category, which led Sequoia to Meituan-Dianping, where consumers order such edibles as desserts and fresh fruit from restaurants and stores and receive delivery from third-party couriers.

Other Sequoia markets were enabled by China's adoption of mobile payments. That's how bike sharing arose. A user could scan a QR code with a smartphone to unlock a bike and make a payment through Alipay or WeChat. Sequoia's experience with investments in ecommerce and mobile payments eased its early bet on Mobike, a Chinese bike-sharing company now operating in over 200 cities.

Meituan's founder, Xing Wang, recalled being impressed with how Shen wielded his operational knowledge when they first met. "He didn't even ask me to talk about my business plan. He had a clear understanding of our business model. That judgment rivaled even that of entrepreneurs in the business."[9]

Sequoia with Chinese Characteristics

Though Sequoia China was rooted in Sequoia's US business, it wasn't controlled by its parent in the traditional way, with big decisions made in California and orders emanating from there. Leone insisted Shen and his team make their own decisions. That was a lesson he'd learned in Israel. When Sequoia and Cisco set up an Israeli investment fund in 1999, their approach was to let the Israelis vet potential deals but have the US office make the decisions. That arrangement proved sluggish. In China, Leone wanted decentralization. Shen was expected to create his own distinctive plan.

Shen's departures from Sequoia's US investment strategy started early. Initially, he and his team financed Qihoo360, an internet security company, and Dianping, a restaurant review site—choices consistent with the focus of Sequoia US. But then they bet on Noah, a wealth management company with no particular enabling technology, investing about $5 million for roughly a 20% stake. Three years later, in 2010, Noah went public on the New York Stock Exchange and raised $100 million. Today it's the largest independent wealth management company in China and valued at $2.6 billion. As the only institutional investor, Sequoia China earned a good return. "You would never have done that without a localized strategy," Shen said. Though Sequoia US had invested in the financial sector, it focused mainly on financial technologies, so-called fintech. But Shen knew his home market well enough to bet not just on IT and health care but also on a broader spectrum of industries, as China was—and still is—in many categories "an open space," he said.

As the market evolved, Sequoia China's strategy diverged further from its parent's. Chinese entrepreneurs, after years of learning from Western peers and being called copycats, had started to develop their own products and business models that didn't have a model in the United States. These companies could baffle even sophisticated investors from Silicon Valley, including Leone himself. For the first 10 years he visited China, while Chinese entrepreneurs were playing catch-up, Leone would point to a Chinese company and say: "I know it—I saw this in the US." Yet over the years, his déjà vu began to fade.

Take Meituan-Dianping as an example of how China is creating new categories of companies. It's hard to define what Meituan-Dianping is. It's a group-buying and review site. It handles food delivery, hotel bookings, movie ticketing, ride hailing, and other services. In 2018, it acquired Mobike. It rolls the services of Groupon, Yelp, Grubhub, Kayak, and Uber into a single enterprise. When Sequoia China first encountered Meituan-Dianping, it was two separate companies: Groupon-like Meituan and Yelp-like Dianping. (Dianping was founded in 2003, a year before Yelp.)

Sequoia China was the only investor in both companies' earliest financing rounds. With the evolution of both—Meituan added food delivery, Dianping started offering group deals—a fight for market share erupted. Both firms burned through cash. Sequoia China facilitated a truce and a merger, which created a company with over 300 million Chinese users. During the company's fund-raising, one leading investor dropped out after its letter of intent was signed. Sequoia China responded by doubling down. It eventually put in a total of $400 million, even though Meituan-Dianping still operates at a loss and some analysts doubt it will ever turn a profit. Shen explained his rationale: "The low logistics costs in China, coupled with high-density cities, is likely to produce massive and successful companies in on-demand services. That's very Chinese. That kind of opportunity is rare in the US."

Pinduoduo is another example. Founded in 2015 by Colin Huang, formerly of Google, the ecommerce company grew in three years from inception to IPO. It resembles Alibaba and JD.com, offering everything from clothing and cosmetics to groceries to home appliances. At first glance, it may seem imprudent to bet on an upstart like this when Alibaba and JD.com control over 70% of Chinese ecommerce. Shen thought the same—at first. But Pinduoduo set itself apart through its social functions. Users can share Pinduoduo's product information on WeChat or QQ, China's dominant social media apps, and get extremely low prices as a result of group buying. For example, a summer dress might be sold initially for the equivalent of $5. But if you and five friends each buy one, you might get them for $1.50 apiece. Pinduoduo's interactive shopping, coupled with low prices, earned it a place in China's ecommerce crowd. Four and a half months after the company launched, it had attracted 10 million users. Three years in, it had 300 million. Now it's the second-largest ecommerce site in China in terms of active users and market value, behind only Alibaba. Initially, its users were primarily women from lower-tier cities (relatively less developed and less populated cities). "It turns out that there are still opportunities for ecommerce penetration in the tier-3 and tier-4 cities with users who have never shopped on Alibaba," Shen said. That surprised even him. And Sequoia China bet correctly: Pinduoduo's IPO on the Nasdaq in 2018 raised $1.6 billion.

Sequoia China's other successes include DJI, the largest drone company in the world; Bytedance, a company that owns a news app, Toutiao, and a video app, TikTok; VIPKid, an online education company connecting Chinese students with overseas teachers; Innovent; and ZaiLabs and Betta, homegrown pharmaceutical companies. That's a broader scope of companies than the parent invests in, and because the China team covers that broader range of industries, it's now bigger than its US counterpart.

Principles Written in Pen

Seeing his China team invest differently doesn't bother Leone. He never doubted that decentralization would result in a drift in strategy. He said he was confident that Sequoia's principles would continue to bind the geographic units together—not just China but also India, Israel, and Southeast Asia. Those principles are "written in pen," meaning not subject to change and accepted across the globe. Number one is "performance transcends time and everything else." As long as that principle is the polestar, the particulars of Shen's moves—investing in a restaurant chain in Chengdu or a video app that live streams guys eating noodles—don't worry Leone. The focus on performance will keep Shen on track.

Then there's trust, which Leone believes he and his Chinese partners have built over their 15 years together. He trusts Shen to run Sequoia China, and Shen has largely maintained his team since the China outfit's founding. The reason, according to Leone, is how Shen manages his people: "He runs a democracy in decision-making and in compensation." In an industry known for big egos, backstabbing, and bitter feuds, Sequoia China's approach is an exception. Tao Zhang, founder of Dianping and a venture investor himself, offered perspective: "In China, most VC [venture capital] firms are a one-man shop. You have this dominant partner, and everyone else works for him. Sequoia China does it in a more institutional way. Neil runs the firm, but he definitely doesn't make all the decisions himself."[10] That appeals to the young talent he needs to keep.

Filaments Woven Together

Beyond the principles, what gives Leone confidence in the ability of the China operation to work in harmony with the rest of the firm is what he calls "many filaments"—the many strands that tie the firm together. No one strand is decisive, but together they bind.

Twice-a-year global leadership meetings are one filament; the company's annual meeting is another. The teams from the various offices traveling together internationally is yet another. An eight-day cross-border trip for young staffers is still another. With each of these, the Sequoia people meet in person and come to understand each other's countries, business context, and approaches. "It incurs costs, but we are committed to it," Shen said. He was referring not so much to cash but rather to opportunity cost—time spent away from finding and developing companies. After COVID-19 erupted in China in December 2019, Sequoia had to put many of these activities on hold and compensated with online Zoom meetings, making sure the global team stayed informed and connected. They even moved their twice-a-year limited partners meeting online.

When the pandemic spread from China, staffers at Sequoia China shared their portfolio companies' experiences of dealing with the crisis with entrepreneurs in India, Southeast Asia, and the United States. "It turns out that entrepreneurs, no matter where they are, face similar challenges under the pandemic," said Xing Liu, one of Sequoia China's partners.[11] "We passed along some of the solutions and approaches that Chinese entrepreneurs adopted and found useful." Because of Sequoia China's alert, Sequoia US became one of the first venture firms to act, issuing the letter "Coronavirus: The Black Swan of 2020" on March 5, 2020, when the United States had confirmed just 11 COVID-19 deaths and few in the country realized the massive impact from the virus.

Another important filament is integration of financial interests. International venture capital firms are not typically a single legal entity. Yet the filaments tie Sequoia's entities together financially. All Sequoia partners are essentially investors in all of the Sequoia affiliated funds: A partner often invests his or her own cash in funds controlled by partners in another region.

On top of this, the limited partners in the many Sequoia funds overlap. That is, the universities, pension funds, and other large institutional investors invest in both Sequoia's US and Chinese funds. This weaving of interests induces that collection of independent legal entities to act more collaboratively than a hierarchical multinational corporation. "There is no such thing as motherhood," said Shen, referring to an eternal right to the profits of Sequoia's offspring. "It has to be two ways, meaning that it's not just the US sharing in the success of China, India and Southeast Asia but also vice versa."

Leone summarized the situation slightly differently: "Nobody has his hands in anybody's pocket." Maybe a better way to say it would be everyone has their hands in everyone's pockets.

This unusual combination of decentralization and centralization works well for Sequoia. Investment and operational decision-making and operations happen at the regional office. Finance, IT, and organizational coordination are centralized in the United States. Yet the seemingly simply setup is hard to execute. "It requires a huge amount of effort and step-by-step everyday practice," Shen said.

Even Leone, the original evangelist of local autonomy, has struggled with letting go at times. For instance, when it comes to decision-making, he never wants the China team to feel as if the US office is dictating to them. But he also feels he has learned a few things in his 30 years of investing, which could help them and which he wants to share. Sequoia's Liu said: "Our US partners are culturally sensitive. They would say: 'This is what we think, but that's from the perspective of Americans. It may not be relevant to your case.'"[12]

There have been times when Leone saw his Chinese partners do something he regarded as odd or ill considered, and he'd pick up the phone and interrogate them until he realized there was logic behind the decision. Now when he sees something he doesn't understand, he tells himself, "There must be a good reason." There usually is, but when crises do arise, as inevitably happens, he usually gets a call from his Chinese partners immediately. "It's not like I find out later that they screwed up and they were trying to fix it," he said.

It's been 15 years since that bright day at that San Francisco hotel, when Leone and Moritz met Shen, and "things have worked terrifically so far," Leone said. When asked how much Sequoia China's success relates to the person he and Moritz handpicked 15 years ago, he pauses for a few seconds: "We got lucky with him. He got lucky with us."

Applying the Framework

Sequoia China is now as economically significant as its US parent. By that measure, it may be the most successful case in this book—perhaps even one of the most successful foreign firms to venture to China. The decisive factors in Sequoia's success were the following:

- Unprecedented growth in demand for venture financing in China provided a brisk economic tailwind for Sequoia and its peers.
- The critical alpha asset Sequoia brought to China was its brand. As a top-tier venture firm that backed a number of legendary Silicon Valley companies, the Sequoia name resonated with Chinese entrepreneurs. Today, Sequoia is to Chinese entrepreneurs what Louis Vuitton is to affluent Chinese shoppers. Those in China who think they're building the next world-changing company believe taking an investment from Sequoia will help make that happen. The brand halo extends to employees those entrepreneurs seek to hire.

Table 6.1: Summary of Success Factors for Sequoia

Factor		Explanation
Demand	▲▲▲	Sequoia bet correctly that venture capital would become important in China. Booming entrepreneurship there propelled Sequoia's success.
Access to market		Sequoia was formed as a separate Chinese entity, which was allowed by the government, but with cross sharing of profits with partners globally.
Advantage	▲▲▲	As a venture firm that had backed a number of legendary Silicon Valley companies, the Sequoia name resonated in China.
Commitment		Sequoia committed a first fund of $160 million, and Sequoia has kept betting on China with additional funds.
Governance	▲▲▲	Shared values, culture, and commitment unite the whole organization. Sequoia let Shen and his team do their work with little interference—but with much support.
Leadership	▲▲▲	As the founding partner of Sequoia China, Neil Shen turned out to be critical.
Strategy		Globally consistent strategy—investors with deep operating experience.
Product		Venture capital is relatively similar worldwide.
Agility	▲▲▲	Sufficient agility from autonomy granted to the China unit.
Luck	▲	Sequoia was lucky to see demand for venture capital boom and in its selection of a China leader.

Note: Upward-pointing triangles indicate a positive factor. Downward-pointing triangles indicate a negative factor. The number of triangles is our subjective assessment of the relative importance of the factor. We omit indicators for those factors that we do not believe were significant for this case.

A Sequoia investment is a signal of quality, increasing the willingness of potential employees, partners, and suppliers to take a risk on a start-up. As with any prestigious brand, a virtuous cycle can emerge: Sequoia's involvement increases the likelihood of a start-up's success, and that success further enhances the brand.

- Sequoia's governance has played a critical role in its success. Investment decisions are made locally, with input from global partners. However, Sequoia deliberately weaves cultural filaments across the firm, including the clear articulation of some principles "written in pen." Reciprocal sharing of financial interests across the partners in all regions ensures team members act as one.

- As the founding partner of Sequoia China, Neil Shen turned out to be critical. The fact that he has risen to become one of the three global stewards at Sequoia also demonstrates his impact at the parent organization. Sequoia's strategy was to pick the right China head and let him and his team do their work with little interference—but much support. This strategy proved highly effective. Even so, recruiting someone from outside is always uncertain, and Sequoia was lucky in its choice.

These elements and other factors in the framework are noted in Table 6.1, along with our subjective assessment of the decisive factors.

In the next chapter, we turn to InMobi, an Indian start-up that broke through China's internet firewall and went on to build a sustainable success.

Chapter 7

InMobi
Jockey or Horse?

In September 2003, Naveen Tewari arrived at Harvard Business School with no intention of starting a business. He'd grown up in a family of academics, attended the Indian Institute of Technology, and then worked at McKinsey in Mumbai for three years. His aim was respectability, not risk taking. Like many of his peers in consulting, he believed an MBA was a safe and prudent way to progress, though he wasn't sure where the degree would take him.

Down the Charles River, at Massachusetts Institute of Technology, Jessie Yang had just entered her second year at the Sloan School of Management. Unlike Tewari, she was crystal clear on her aim: "I always wanted to be a CEO, running a business in China."[1] She'd put that statement in her application essay for Sloan.

During those days in Boston, neither of them knew that someday their paths would cross through a company called InMobi— today the world's largest independent mobile advertising network, valued at over $1 billion and one of the very few foreign internet firms that have succeeded in China. Tewari founded InMobi in his home country, and Yang ended up leading the firm in China.

A Start-Up's Global Ambition

Tewari's time at Harvard transformed his ambitions. He met a bunch of entrepreneurs who visited campus as speakers and mentors. Then came a summer internship with a venture capital firm, Charles River Ventures, which exposed him to the world of start-ups. He was hooked.

By the end of 2006, he'd returned to India. The following year, he persuaded three of his friends—Mohit Saxena, Amit Gupta, and Abhay Singhal—to launch a text-messaging-powered search business, which he called mKhoj. To access mKhoj's service, a consumer needed to type key search words, such as the product and the location, and SMS (send a text message over a mobile phone) into mKhoj. The results would be a collection of deals for that product nearby. That venture didn't take off, and Tewari shut it down within six months. "We were betting against macro," he said. "The fact that the internet was going to take off meant that the SMS would go down. The SMS might be a good business, but it would never become large."[2] Tewari wanted big. At the time, the iPhone had just debuted, and the mobile web was showing early signs of promise. He and his friends decided to try a mobile advertising network—a platform connecting advertisers and publishers to serve ads to consumers—and changed their venture's name to InMobi.

From the very beginning, Tewari knew India was a small market for mobile advertising. To really grow, he and his friends had to take InMobi overseas. They first went to neighboring Southeast Asia ("a large market with an easy access") and then Africa and the Middle East ("no competition"). Then came the United Kingdom. Tewari waited until InMobi had built a large share in its other markets before entering the United States, the largest advertising market. "If we went there early, we would be beaten up," he said. By 2011, InMobi had expanded into over five countries across five continents and employed around 350 people.

As Tewari was plotting out the early years of InMobi, Yang too was experiencing ups and downs. After Sloan, she'd returned home to China and landed a job with McKinsey. She hadn't relinquished her CEO dream, but she said she felt as if 10 years in the United States had estranged her from her homeland. She wanted to reconnect with her fellow Chinese before trying to run a business of her own. She stayed at McKinsey for three years. Then a classmate from Sloan invited her to join a start-up called Sky Flying Media Group, an advertising firm, and she became the COO. The company raised $81 million from investors like Sequoia Capital and Goldman Sachs but never managed to do the IPO its executive team envisioned.

On December 31, 2011—a day she remembers vividly—a headhunter called, asking whether she'd be interested in a general manager position at a mobile advertising company. Though the headhunter didn't disclose the employer, she figured it out. A few months prior, in September, InMobi had made headlines worldwide when Softbank pumped $200 million into the four-year-old firm, then one of the biggest investments in the mobile internet. With that trove of cash on hand, Tewari was making a play for China, a notoriously difficult market for foreign internet companies. eBay, Yahoo, Google, and Groupon had all flopped there; Groupon didn't even last a year. "Everybody told us not to go to China," Tewari said. But the Chinese market was just too enticing, with its 900 million mobile phone users;[3] it was the second-largest market for the iPhone and the largest market for smartphones overall. By the time Tewari's headhunter identified Yang, InMobi had been running in China for a few tough months. "It was complex," he recalled. "You got there and didn't know what's happening. Totally different language and different people." He'd hired a sales manager to lead a team of 20, but that wasn't working out. He figured he needed someone with a global perspective and local roots, someone who was "looking to make a mark." Yang clearly fit that description, but Tewari was concerned that someone with her credentials wouldn't risk her career on a still largely unknown company. At the time, developed-world multinationals were scooping up the best talent in China.

His worries were unfounded. Yang met the team and was impressed. "They were so smart and so energetic—they really wanted to get things done," she said. They soon cut a deal.

Transforming the Typical China Branch

What Yang inherited was a typical multinational firm's China branch. Employees came from everywhere: China, of course, as well as Taiwan, Hong Kong, Canada, and Korea. They may not have been skilled at their jobs, but they had one thing in common: They spoke good English. That was essential for communicating with their bosses in Bangalore. "There was no collaboration within the China team," Yang said. And the pace was slow—"everybody had an easy life."

Outside the company, the scene differed. Though mobile advertising was nascent, start-ups were popping up willy-nilly. "There were more than 100 companies competing with us," said Yang. These were primarily venture-funded Chinese firms—they were agile and understood the market. Coming out of McKinsey and a failed start-up, Yang remembered feeling a little intimidated. She wasn't well connected with her new peers in Chinese tech companies. "I was pretty much nobody." Plus, her stint with McKinsey had marked her as a corporate type, someone content with routine and wary of risk. She set out to prove that image wrong. She spent her days meeting with potential clients and her evenings firing off emails. She recalls feeling grateful when she got to bed before 2 a.m. "It was really hard for her," said Tawari. "But she took it and grew the business bigger and bigger."

InMobi's product, an intermediary between advertisers and publishers, helped. Advertisers are brands, such as Procter & Gamble, L'Oréal, or Nike, and publishers are websites or mobile apps that host ads. InMobi aggregates publishers and packages their ads based on certain parameters, then sells the packages to advertisers. It profits from the difference between what it pays publishers for advertising space and what it receives from advertisers. InMobi was the first ad-tech company in China that introduced a platform for native ads (ads that don't really look like ads but blend into the environment in which they're placed). The look, feel, and function of the ads match that of other items on the publisher's site or app. Such an ad might just look like a piece of news in a news app or a social feed on a social media site. It's less intrusive and more likely to pull users in. Before the native ad platform appeared in 2014, InMobi's products were mainly banner ads and interstitials, but it had still managed to find an edge over competitors with better ad targeting. "If you were hungry and an ad of a restaurant nearby popped up on your phone, would you click?" asked Kevin Wang, InMobi China's marketing head.[4] In many cases, the answer was yes. InMobi had been using machine learning to deliver the right ad at the right time. In other words, it was making ads more relevant. That's something all advertisers strive for but don't necessarily achieve.

InMobi's biggest global competitor was Google. Google introduced native ads in China a few years after InMobi had done so. After it moved its Chinese-language search engine to Hong Kong, its mainland China business back then was mainly "outbound," meaning it helped Chinese advertisers target international audiences. That left space for InMobi to thrive in China's massive domestic market.

Yang, for her part, had learned a great deal from her previous disappointments, and she put those lessons to work in her new job. "If I joined InMobi right after McKinsey, I don't know if I could make it successful," she said. In the two months after she took over, she hired 20 sales reps and charged them with identifying the right customers for InMobi. At the time, there were two kinds of customers in the mobile advertising world that sales reps tried to avoid. Firms in the first group didn't have the budget for InMobi's services but pretended they did to get a peek at the latest ad technology. Firms in the second group had the budget, but their products weren't suitable for mobile promotion.

InMobi's sales reps, over time, learned to weed out those kinds of customers and move quickly to high-potential leads. Today, InMobi's customers include some of China's leading companies: ecommerce giant JD.com, retailer Suning, and ride-hailing company Didi Chuxing. Compensation for InMobi's sales reps reflected their contributions to the company, something that wasn't always true at the multinationals in China. Starting in the 1990s, multinationals had attracted employees as they do everywhere—through competitive salaries and benefits and the promise of job security. But the rise of Chinese companies, especially internet firms, which often rewarded top performers with heftier pay and generous stock options, dimmed the multinationals' allure. Rigid corporate compensation systems even inspired the invention of a term of derision: "capitalism big pot," derived from "communism big pot," meaning everybody at a multinational firm received equal pay, regardless of his or her contribution. That sort of structure drove away ambitious risk takers. At InMobi, sales reps were compensated on commission from day one: the more deals they closed, the more they earned. "As a start-up, we needed to hire hungry sales people," Yang said. In 2013, a year after Yang joined, InMobi China increased its revenue tenfold.[5]

Once customers were locked in, they showed unusual tolerance for InMobi's mistakes. Early on, its platform crashed, which would've been a disaster and an embarrassment if it had happened in the United States or Japan. But customers didn't leave. "The Chinese market is not about perfection," Yang said. "Even if your product isn't mature, your clients still want to test it out. What they want is speed—get the product out first and then improve it along the way."

Unusual Product Localization

To tailor its product to China, InMobi has undergone three stages of localization. In the first, it offered the globally standardized ad platform with minor adjustments. "We only had one product team in Bangalore, and we only localized the language for China," Tewari said. Soon it became clear that wouldn't work in China.

In the United States, InMobi had partnered with Rubicon Project to build InMobi Exchange, a platform that enables the use of software to purchase online ads (as opposed to the traditional way, where ad buyers and sellers negotiate to get deals done). Rubicon operated in countries such as the United Kingdom, Australia, and Japan—but not China. Plus, Yang's China team wanted their own local product, not something developed by a third party. So engineers in Bangalore got to work and created one. The product worked so well that other regions picked it up too, even InMobi US. Few foreign companies have been willing to make a product just for China. But for InMobi, China mattered mightily: It generated one-quarter of the ad tech company's global sales. Tewari had to keep pouring in resources.

When InMobi entered China, the local internet giants weren't committed to mobile. Baidu, Tencent, and Alibaba were born in the desktop era. Though they'd watched the rise of the mobile internet and even developed products, they were still experimenting and testing. Many of their products weren't designed with a mobile-first mind-set. Yet a couple of years in, they all realized mobile would replace the web as the main way consumers accessed the internet in China. When that happened, InMobi began to feel pressure. "We can't compete with BAT on scale," Yang said, referring to the three companies as an acronym. "But we can be faster than them, releasing products a few quarters ahead of them."

InMobi's engineers in Bangalore strived to stay ahead, but they found themselves whipsawed between China speed and the more methodical pace of the rest of the world. "Global markets often have a one-year product road map, but Chinese companies have a three-month road map," Tewari said. "They always launch, launch, and launch. If a product fails, they don't care. If it succeeds, they do it more. They just move fast." When he met with Chinese clients and partners, he'd hear they wanted to move even faster; they wanted new products, new features, and faster rollout. In other markets, the pace was slower. Engineers would lavish time on details, making sure everything was right before releasing a product to the market. "China wants speed. The global market wants perfection. When you have the two things, they collide with each other," he said.

Working fast created internal frictions, exacerbating the language and cultural differences between Bangalore and Beijing. The China team and Indian engineers in Bangalore worked hard at communication, but, with China racing ahead in the mobile internet, the two teams were often out of sync. As a result, Tewari decided to let InMobi China form its own product team and design products specifically for China. "We had asked for it for three years," Yang said. That product team now works in the Beijing office, and its 40 members build "whatever they want to build," according to Tewari. Their data are stored in InMobi China's data center in Beijing, as opposed to on Microsoft's Azure, the choice in InMobi's other markets.

By October 2019, one-quarter of Chinese customers were using InMobi's China-exclusive products. "But two years from now, I think it will be 100%," Tewari said. He said he regretted not making the transition earlier. "I kept China on the global platform too long." China generated around $100 million in revenue for InMobi annually, and Tewar wanted to double and even triple that quickly. He knew this wouldn't happen if he didn't unshackle his China team. "If we want China to do $500 million in three years, how will it do it on a same global platform? You have to give China everything."

The Chinese Way

Having its own product team is just one way InMobi China operates differently from InMobi's businesses elsewhere. It also has an independent strategy, one that's consistent with those in other markets but not determined by them. In advertising, there's an ongoing debate over whether to focus on the supply side (the publishers) or the demand side (the advertisers). InMobi China picked the supply side from the beginning and has stuck with it. Yang's logic is this: Internet traffic is the foundation, and the business monetizes that traffic. So recruiting high-quality publishers is her top priority. Once that high-quality supply is secured, it attracts demand; advertisers care about whether their ads are displayed on channels that will generate the results they want.

InMobi China is also selective about the advertisers it works with, contracting only with premium ones, which ensures high-quality ads. Premium clients often develop better ads, thus delivering a better experience for users of the publisher's site or app. The users are then more likely to engage with the ads. A virtuous circle ensues: High-quality publishers attract better ads and more consumers, which brings in more publishers.

Still, Bangalore did develop global strategies and asked each region to follow through. That's what a smart headquarters does, using centralized management to gain benefits of scale or cost efficiency. But in China, many of these initiatives encountered resistance. One spat arose over ad campaign management. InMobi services its clients through sales reps and campaign managers. Sales reps set out to understand customer needs and meet them. Campaign managers, on the other hand, run the ad campaigns for customers. They work closely with customers, setting up campaign strategies, tracking performance, and optimizing results. They often handle tricky situations, like seemingly unreasonable customer requests. A customer might tell a campaign manager: "We are going to run a campaign tomorrow, and we don't have all the materials needed yet, but we're going live tomorrow!" The campaign manager, instead of flatly turning down the customer, tries to make this work. InMobi's headquarters, at one point, wanted to centralize campaign management in Bangalore. It thought this would dramatically cut costs. Yang balked; Bangalore insisted. Yang kept pushing back, and eventually her bosses relented. InMobi China was the only region that didn't implement the strategy. "They probably felt I was difficult to work with, but I just wanted to do the right thing for the business," she said. "They would understand when they saw the results." Those results came a couple of years later. InMobi China had continued to thrive while other regions, especially non-English-speaking countries, like Japan and Korea, had suffered. InMobi Japan and Korea wound up rehiring their campaign managers.

Yang said her job requires that she be willing to speak out when she thinks her bosses are wrong. Her Chinese roots have given her a deeper knowledge of her market than her colleagues in India. What's more, as a former consultant, she has seen multinationals fail in China. She said she believed one of the reasons for these failures is that local staffers deferred too much to headquarters, even when they knew global strategies didn't make much sense for China. So when her turn came, she was willing to argue (though she picked her fights judiciously). She was often right, and that built her credibility within the larger organization. "Autonomy is earned," she said.

"Jessie is practical," said Kevin Wang. "She knows when to be tough, when to soften. She can get things done." This applies to not only how she acts within the organization but also how she navigates outside. InMobi competes with Baidu, Alibaba, and Tencent head-to-head, yet it also collaborates with them. Some of their apps, such as Baidu Video and QQ music, are part of InMobi's platform. How could they not be? InMobi is the biggest independent ad network in China, partnering with over 30,000 apps and covering 80% of iOS users and 40% of Android users.

Unshackling China

Yang conceded InMobi China wouldn't have achieved this without Tewari. By all accounts, Tewari is unusually open-minded. Every time he travels to China, he meets with at least 10 customers. He wants to know them and what they want from InMobi. "They will tell you what they need," he said. "Once you understand what they need, you just give it to them." When it comes to China, he said he's developed a looser approach to management: "You have to let it be loose about what your culture is and what you do here." He lets InMobi China operate like a start-up. All the reporting lines go through Yang. He has let her create a local corporate culture, and he doesn't mind InMobi losing its identity as an Indian company. He wants to blend in. "A lot of people in China think we are a Chinese company, which is exactly what we want," he said.

InMobi China has done well enough—and differs enough from its parent and peers—that Tewari has even decided to spin it off, making it an independent company that, in theory, can grow even faster. He said he aimed to "unshackle" it. This is, needless to say, an unusual decision for a foreign internet company—maybe an unprecedented one. The company originally planned to make it happen in 2020, yet decided to postpone due to the COVID-19 pandemic. But the China unit is already running independently.

Once InMobi China becomes an independent company, Yang will have realized her CEO dream, and Tewari's creation will have become the first foreign internet company to achieve real success in China.

Applying the Framework

The Chinese internet market has been notoriously difficult for foreign players to break into. These factors were critical to InMobi's ability to do what many bigger, older firms couldn't:

- InMobi came to China with one clear advantage: Its product, though imperfect, outperformed those of Chinese start-ups. This is the same advantage any hot start-up has when seizing an opportunity created by a new technology. But product superiority is fleeting. Competitors will respond very quickly. As China's internet giants jumped into mobile, InMobi responded by not only becoming even more agile (that is, by releasing products more frequently) but also developing other alpha assets. One was its customer network. InMobi bet on the supply side, recruiting a vast network of high-quality publishers. Those publishers, of course, attracted more advertisers, creating that virtuous circle. Accompanying that growing network is an increasingly visible brand. InMobi now is no longer a small Indian start-up but rather a well-known brand associated with innovation.
- Tewari was flexible with his company's governance to accommodate his China unit's needs. Initially, the company was headquarters-centered, with each function reporting back to India, little different from other multinationals. But as Yang built credibility, InMobi China gained rare autonomy.

Table 7.1: Summary of Success Factors for InMobi

Factor		Explanation
Demand	▲▲	Very rapidly growing mobile computing ecosystem in China.
Access to market		No significant barriers to a wholly owned foreign entity entering mobile advertising.
Advantage	▲	Initial product advantage, with a transition to customer network as the primary alpha asset.
Commitment		As China became increasingly important to InMobi's global revenue, the company kept injecting capital and giving the China unit the resources needed to maintain momentum. Now, China constitutes 40% of the company's total investments on sales and operations.
Governance	▲▲▲	Tewari granted substantial autonomy and eventually allowed a nearly completely local product.
Leadership	▲▲▲	Yang proved a skilled leader, bringing the right mix of a consultant's insight discipline and an entrepreneur's drive.
Strategy	▲	InMobi's strategy was to leverage its established technology to gain a foothold in China and then build local advantages as the company grew there. It succeeded so well on that score that it's now spinning off its China unit.
Product	▲	InMobi has gone through three stages of product localization—from the initial language-only localization, to developing a product for China, to eventually hiring a separate Chinese product team to build "whatever they want." That effort to achieve on product-market fit is rare.
Agility	▲▲	Yang was an entrepreneur at heart and was given autonomy from headquarters. She could act with the speed of a local entrepreneur.
Luck	▲	Yang exceeded expectations and thus proved to be a lucky choice for a leader.

Note: Upward-pointing triangles indicate a positive factor. Downward-pointing triangles indicate a negative factor. The number of triangles is our subjective assessment of the relative importance of the factor. We omit indicators for those factors that we do not believe were significant for this case.

That wasn't guaranteed; her early successes and the significant sales growth won the trust of her bosses. As Yang summarizes the situation: "Autonomy is not awarded but gained."

- InMobi's success is closely tied to its local leadership. Yang turned out to be a rare fit for her firm. Her previous failure taught her lessons, which applied to InMobi. Having witnessed foreign multinationals' mistakes in China in her position as a consultant, she aimed not to repeat them. Many of her strategies, from compensation to product localization, though different from InMobi's global standard practices, fit the local conditions. With her consistently strong performance, she has risen to become one of the key executives at InMobi global.

These elements and other factors in the framework are noted in Table 7.1, along with our subjective assessment of the decisive factors.

We now turn to the story of Intel, a company whose alpha asset of indispensable product technology proved to be decisive in its success.

Chapter 8

Intel
Alpha Chips

In January 2019, Robert Swan was allowed to drop "interim" from his title—he became the permanent CEO at Intel. In April, only a few months after that announcement, he flew to China, where he first used his official Chinese name, Si Ruibo. He met with the vice minister of industry and information technology, a tradition for Intel executives (whenever they visit China, they schedule time with government officials, even if the meetings seem symbolic). And he convened Intel's Chinese employees, who were eager to hear their new boss's plans for their home country. Ian Yang, Intel China president, recalled: "Our CEO told us to dive deep in the demand of Chinese market."[1] Yang interpreted this as a charge to create a customized strategy for China and not just copy Intel's global strategy.

If you are wondering why one country, even one as large as China, deserves special attention from the new CEO of one of the world's leading semiconductor makers, consider this: Despite trade tensions between China and the United States, China still delivered $20.16 billion in annual revenue for Intel in 2019, more than one-quarter of the company's $72 billion total.[2] That poses an obvious question: How did one of the oldest, most respected firms in Silicon Valley thrive in a country that seems to favor agile upstarts?

A Pioneer's Long-Awaited Opportunity

Intel opened its first China office in Beijing in 1985, amid an early wave of foreign investment. Like many of its peers, the chip giant didn't make much progress there at first. China's economy had only recently opened to the rest of the world, and Western investments were typically small. Mostly, Intel waited and watched from its office at the National Palace Hotel.

In 1992, Deng Xiaoping, the Chinese leader who had initiated his country's economic reforms, took a tour of the southern cities that were thriving thanks to their burgeoning economies—Shenzhen, Zhuhai, and Shanghai. Throughout the trip, Deng boasted of the region's economic accomplishments while deriding his critics. The publicity around the trip and Deng's pointed remarks reinvigorated economic reform in China, which had been imperiled by the 1989 political turmoil. Foreign companies, especially IT firms, entered a new phase of growth in China. US PC makers AST and Compaq built factories. IBM added Shanghai and Guangzhou branches in addition to its Beijing headquarters. Hewlett-Packard started transforming its Chinese joint venture, introducing a more Western-style operational model. And Motorola invested $120 million in a plant in Tianjian, as its pagers became a hit among China's emerging consumer class.[3] That year, China attracted more foreign direct investment than any other developing country.[4]

Andy Grove, then Intel's CEO, visited China the following year. After his trip, he and the rest of Intel's management team concluded that Intel would, in time, thrive in China. "Everybody we met at government was single-minded and determined and generally very well informed on technology," Sean Maloney, then Grove's technical assistant, recalled about the trip. "Many governments elsewhere were ambivalent or uninformed. Here was a series of local and central officials who had a single purpose, which was to develop the country around a strong technology base."[5] And China was eager to welcome Western technology giants like Intel. It had begun to try to build its own semiconductor industry in the early 1990s but had not yet made real progress.

Intel redoubled its efforts in China. It appointed Wee Theng Tan, its director of business operations for Asia Pacific, who was ethnically Chinese and had grown up in Singapore, as its country manager and sent Jason Chen, a Taiwanese sales manager, to build out its distribution network. It also dispatched Jim Jarrett, an executive at Intel's headquarters, in Santa Clara, California, to be the company's first China president. Tan recalled how Andy Grove and Paul Otellini, then the CEO and senior vice president, respectively, had persuaded him to take his China post: "China is going to be the next big thing for Intel. If you want to do something about it, come over to China."[6] That was 1996, and Intel China's revenue was only about $75 million, less than 1% of the company's total. Tan wasn't sure, but his bosses were adamant.

Betting on Underdogs

In the middle of the 1990s, personal computers were luxury items in China, often priced around 15,000 RMB ($1,800)—more than a year's salary for someone in a top-tier city like Beijing and Shanghai. Foreign brands, including IBM, Compaq, and Hewlett-Packard, dominated the market, and their computers were Intel's main source of revenue. Lenovo, now the world's largest PC maker, and other Chinese manufacturers accounted for only 10% of PC sales. Though Intel's top management believed PCs would come to be used by everyone in China, the high price made that vision initially unrealistic. Intel's executives in China realized that, to make their bosses' vision a reality, they needed to make PCs affordable for more of the Chinese people. "If you tell consumers to buy an IBM PC, the price is too high, and the entry barrier for consumers is too steep," Tan said. "The locals are able to make PCs with the same functionality at less than half of the price."

Since the sky-high prices were the biggest hurdle for PC demand and foreign brands were often sold at even higher prices than local brands, Intel China predicted that the local manufacturers would come to dominate the industry in China. So it decided to help along the development of local manufacturers, providing central processing units (CPUs) at reasonable prices, which would enable Chinese manufacturers to compete with foreign brands and consumers could buy PCs at reasonable prices. That was a bold move, given that the most profitable local PC maker, Lenovo, sold only an average of 100,000 units each year. Intel executives at headquarters were initially hesitant, but they gave the China team the go-ahead.

In China, the person tasked to implement the plan was Ian Yang, who had become Intel China's president. Originally from Chongqing, Yang had attended college in the United States in the 1980s. As part of his program, he'd interned at Intel and never left. Upon returning to China in 1995, he wasted no time in cultivating relationships in the fledgling computer industry. At one client meeting, he met Yuanqing Yang, the general manager of Lenovo's PC division. The two hit it off, with Ian frequently visiting Yuanqing at his office.

Intel launched its Pentium series in 1993 and, with the help of Microsoft's Windows operating systems, inaugurated the "Wintel" era. Yet by 1995, all the PC makers in China, foreign and local, were still selling computers with Intel's less powerful 386 or 486 microprocessors. The thinking was that those were good enough for an immature market like China. Ian was determined to persuade Yuanqing to adopt the Pentium for Lenovo's computers. But, after many attempts, his pitch wasn't working. Then one day Yuanqing unexpectedly called to say he was running out of 486 chips and wanted to upgrade. One of the main reasons was Intel had cut the prices of its Pentium chips recently, and Yuanqing saw the opportunity to improve his PCs but still make a profit.[7] The order came with a condition—he wanted a big discount. Ian and Tan had to fly to US headquarters for approval.

In 1996, Lenovo released PCs with Intel's Pentium chips, priced at 10,000 RMB ($1,200). That brought an enthusiastic consumer response: Lenovo sold 240,000 units that year and surpassed Compaq and IBM, becoming the leading PC maker in China, with a 10%

market share.[8] Inspired by Lenovo's success, other local PC makers followed the same strategy. With Intel's support, more local manufacturers sprung up, competing head-to-head with foreign brands. The competition culminated in 2005, when Lenovo acquired IBM's PC division and the famous ThinkPad brand.

Intel's alliance with Lenovo and other Chinese manufacturers went far beyond providing chips. As a well-known multinational, with the admired Grove as its chairman, Intel was often asked by its young Chinese partners for advice. Tan recalled giving talks on handling vendor relationships at Lenovo. He and his colleagues were willing to help out because they believed that building guanxi could only bring benefits.

The emergence of local PC makers and their affordable computers helped increase the Chinese appetite for PCs. Intel, one of a handful of B2B companies that had managed to make itself a household name in the United States, had well-honed skills for pitching to consumers directly and brought those to bear. It threw Chinese "PC parties," marketing events intended to amplify demand.

To educate tech-naive Chinese consumers, Intel would hold the events every weekend, inviting people to play with and learn about computers. Of course, alerting them to "Intel inside"—the company's storied marketing slogan—was an indispensable part of those "educational" sessions. Intel also arranged for local PC manufacturers to sell their products at the events at deep discounts, sometimes half of the market price. The parties drew crowds; one held at the Beijing library attracted over 40,000 people. Another, which took place on one of Chengdu's electronics streets, was attended by over 200,000.[9] Over several years, Intel hosted around 1,000 PC parties in multiple cities.

Tan credited the success to the team's execution—"especially Jason Chen." According to Tan, Chen didn't miss a major PC party. He traveled around China and even to Tibet and stayed in cheap hotels to ensure the parties and other marketing campaigns came off as planned. With his efforts, channel sales grew to be one-third of Intel's revenue. Chen later became a vice president of Intel, overseeing global sales and marketing, and is now CEO of Acer, a Taiwanese electronics company.

Intel had little difficulty attracting talent in China. A Shanghai newspaper once rated it as the most desirable foreign employer in the city. That resulted in a government affairs team that other multinationals envied. Navigating China's nontransparent, unpredictable regulations wasn't easy, said Wangli Moser, a former head of the team, but the one lodestar was to "align your strategy with China's national agenda."[10]

Going West

China had focused economic development on coastal cities, leaving underdeveloped its vast western regions. In 2000, the central government issued a "go west" policy, encouraging domestic and international enterprises to invest in such hinterland hubs as Chengdu, Chognqing, and Xi'an. The majority of multinational companies hugged the urbanized East Coast at the time.

Intel became the first to heed the government's directive. It was already planning an assembly and testing plant in China. It had previously set up a lab and a testing and packaging facility in Shanghai, so Shanghai would've made sense as the location for the plant. But Intel chose Chengdu, 1,000 miles west of Shanghai and with much less developed infrastructure and transportation.

Chengdu was better known as the home of China's famed pandas (the country's research center for panda breeding is there) than as a center of commerce. Intel initially invested $375 million in the plant and then added $150 million and an additional $75 million. When completed in 2005, the plant was the biggest operation by a multinational in Chengdu. Later, it became one of Intel's largest assembly and testing sites—one of every two laptops in the world was configured with a chip processed by this plant. Intel's suppliers, partners, and other multinationals (for example, Lenovo, IBM, Dell, Siemens, Texas Instruments, Philips) also flocked to Chengdu. Even rival Advanced Micro Devices created a research and sales center in the city. These days, Chengdu aspires to be China's Silicon Valley, and its former mayor, Honglin Ge, considers Intel's arrival the impetus of that dream.[11]

Picking Chengdu wasn't just smart politics for Intel; there were financial payoffs of cheap land, lower wages, and a tax reduction. And the political gratitude kept coming. A former Intel China supply-chain executive recalled her negotiations with China Telecom. The state-owned monopoly was known for its bruising negotiations. But the former executive said it took a different approach with Intel. China Telecom asked her what terms Intel wanted and agreed to them—treatment she had never received in other deals she'd handled.

Intel had figured out what the Chinese government valued most—the country's long-term growth—and demonstrated its commitment to that. Intel was rewarded accordingly. In 2015, when its rival, Qualcomm, was fined $975 million for violating China's anti-monopoly law,[12] Intel came away untouched, despite having dominated the Chinese semiconductor industry for decades.

Getting Intel's top executives in California to agree to Chengdu wasn't a sure thing; the company was also considering options in Thailand, Vietnam, and the Philippines. But Tan, by then Intel China's president, kept lobbying in Santa Clara. Often people thousands of miles away can't really understand the on-the-ground reality of a distant and culturally distinct market like China. That can lead to conflicts. Intel was no exception. Tan recalled being challenged or even embarrassed many times. This was, after all, a company whose chairman, Grove, had titled his memoir *Only the Paranoid Survive*. Skeptical questioning was expected. "But you can't be afraid to take the risk, address the senior management team and give them the rationale," Tan said.

Fortunately for Intel, Tan's bosses, especially Grove, retained their faith in China's potential. Tan first met Grove while working as Intel's general manager for Southeast Asia. Shortly afterward, he found himself exchanging emails with Grove, which stunned him after spending 10 years at IBM, a company notorious for its hierarchical reporting lines. Grove encouraged him to be brash. Once Tan was interrupted and ignored while giving a presentation at a senior management meeting at headquarters, and Grove urged him to assert himself, to make sure the view from China was heard. What's more, Grove, who was CEO until 1998 and chairman until 2004, insisted that every board member visit China at least once a year. Though Tan groused about becoming a "travel agency," he knew how valuable it was to have those kinds of relationships. Craig Barrett, Grove's successor as CEO, witnessed a PC party in Chengdu with 200,000 attendees, and Paul Otellini, who took over from Barrett in 2005, became convinced that China was critical to Intel, insulating it against slowdowns in the US market.

China didn't disappoint. The market's growth ratified Intel's bet. In the mid-1990s, the entire country had only about 600,000 PCs. By 2000, that number had jumped to more than 7 million. Then in 2012, China topped the United States as the largest PC market worldwide, with over 66 million shipments. Intel's business in China swelled accordingly, growing from $75 million in 1996 to $20.16 billion in 2019.[13]

Attacks from AMD and China

Of course, China's potential was no secret; it appealed to Intel's rivals too. Advanced Micro Devices, better known as AMD, entered China in 1993 but hedged its commitment. Its management team was primarily based in Hong Kong, leaving only the sales force in mainland China. In 2002, AMD changed strategy, establishing a China headquarters in Beijing and assembling a local team, including a Chinese CEO. It started a price war, forcing Intel to cut prices as much as 30%. It even broke into Intel's longtime partnerships with international brands such as Dell and Hewlett-Packard. They both launched PCs in China with AMD microprocessors. In just a few years, AMD managed to seize 15% of the PC market.

While scrapping with AMD, Intel also found itself in a spat with the Chinese government. In 2004, China announced a homegrown standard for wireless technology: the wired authentication and privacy infrastructure (WAPI). All international companies that sold computers, microprocessors, and other wireless products in China would have to adhere to it and work with Chinese companies selected by the government to implement the standard. "That amounts to opening your chip, and all your intellectual property would be gone," Tan said. Intel opted to resist, announcing it wouldn't provide a WAPI-compliant chipset. Tan and his team spent a year and a half fighting the new standard, and the wrangle eventually landed at the WTO, which adjudicates trade disputes. China ended up dropping the standard. Though Intel won, a rupture had opened between the company and Beijing. To close it, Tan's bosses in California decided to "give China the fab they always wanted."

A "fab" is a semiconductor fabrication plant, and it houses a chip maker's intellectual property. Given China's lack of protection for intellectual property at the time, none of the foreign chip makers had set up fabs there. Intel's fabs were mainly located in Western countries, and a fab required a hefty investment. China had been asking Intel to construct one since the 1990s in hopes of boosting its semiconductor industry, but Intel had held back. In March 2007, it announced it would spend $2.5 billion to build a chip-manufacturing plant in China, then the country's single largest foreign investment to date. Intel again displayed its facility with corporate diplomacy by choosing to locate the plant in Dalian, a northeastern city where the central government had called for investment.

The plant opened three years later with fanfare, but its reality didn't match the public relations. Concerned about its technologies and facing US restrictions on technology exports, Intel had brought to China a technology two generations behind its production processes elsewhere. Its Western factories were producing its most advanced 22-nanometer chips, while the Chinese plant could make only 65-nanometer chips, mainly used for the low end of the market. As Intel upgraded its technology elsewhere, the chips produced in Dalian became obsolete, losing appeal for potential customers. As a result, the plant's output was low, and the large investment didn't yield a return.

Several years later, Intel converted the plant to the production of nonvolatile memory chips, which don't require power to retain data. These chips were widely used in smartphones, tablets, and data centers, a rapidly growing segment in China. As memory chips didn't require the same level of sophistication as microprocessors, the US government didn't restrict technology transfers to the plant. Intel now could take more advanced technologies, such as 3D XPoint, to Dalian and thus compete with Samsung, SK Hynix, and Toshiba, the main players in this field. Nonvolatile memory chips were a small part of Intel's portfolio, accounting for about 6% of total revenue, but the business grew at over 20% in both 2017 and 2018.[14]

Tan left Intel in 2008 after the original Dalian deal. During his 12 years in China, Intel had become one of the most prominent tech companies there. It had committed $4.3 billion to the country, and that investment yielded significant returns. Annual China revenue reached $7.5 billion in 2008, contributing 15%–20% of global revenue. Intel China also employed over 7,000 people in 16 locations. And it was a major venture capital investor, having staked 50 companies, including sohu.com, one of the earliest internet companies in China to go public on NASDAQ. More importantly, it dominated the semiconductor industry, with an approximately 85% market share. The role of AMD, Tan had joked, was to save Intel from accusations of a monopoly. Though AMD had good technology, it hadn't achieved the market acceptance in China that Intel had. Intel had built a brand in China. "When you build brand acceptance, it's not easy for a newcomer to come to your field to knock you off," Tan said.

Intel did make smart choices, but its successes during this period also related to China's stumbles in developing its own semiconductor industry. China's efforts dated back to the 1950s, when the technology was invented in the United States. But in the 1960s and 1970s, the political turmoil known as the Cultural Revolution waylaid the country. Only in the 1990s did the central government begin to try to revitalize the semiconductor industry. The results were lackluster.

Unlike in more basic industries, such as clothing or home appliances, where China quickly caught up, semiconductors required advanced technological capabilities that China didn't have. And it couldn't acquire them from the United States, South Korea, or Japan, as these countries blocked access to their know-how and thwarted Chinese acquisition attempts. A shortage of talent was another problem. China was graduating 500,000 engineering students a year, but few had the background to work in semiconductors. Becoming an expert in semiconductor engineering is a long-term commitment, and China's best engineers saw more immediate returns in the booming internet economy. Making chips also required a massive up-front investment and the financial wherewithal to wait several years to see a return. Chinese companies didn't then have that capacity, and investment from the central government was insufficient and fragmented. At one point, the government had invested in 130 fabrication sites across more than 15 provinces, none of which worked out.[15]

Finding New Territory

More recently, the Chinese semiconductor industry has burgeoned, creating challenges for Intel. Local companies have grown from start-up to sturdy in just a few years. Semiconductor Manufacturing International Corp. (SMIC) in Shanghai has become the world's fourth-largest chip maker in just a few years. Spreadtrum and Hisilicon have risen quickly in chip design. And Chinese demand for chips has swelled, consuming more than half of the world's semiconductors annually. That growth has brought even more competition in the form of such firms as Taiwan Semiconductor Manufacturing Co., a maker of chips for the iPhone and iPad, and Nvidia, a leading chip maker for artificial intelligence.

The Chinese government also has increased its investment in the industry, aiming to create national champions. In 2014, it set up a $21.9 billion investment fund to boost design and manufacturing capabilities. In 2018, after the Trump administration banned US companies from selling components to ZTE, a Chinese telecommunications giant, the fund received $47.4 billion for a second round of investment. It has also taken capital from the private sector and has been run with a market-based approach, with a goal of making profits. China has also been able to attract talent from Taiwan. From 2014 through 2018, nearly 1,000 Taiwanese engineers moved to mainland China.[16] "It's relatively easier to get talent from Taiwan, as we share the same language and culture," said an Intel R&D leader, who spoke on the condition of anonymity.[17]

Intel largely missed out on the mobile revolution globally; Qualcomm still dominates China's mobile market. But Intel has diversified its operations in other areas, including the rapidly growing data-center demand from such leading Chinese internet companies as Alibaba, Tencent, Baidu, and JD.com. The first three companies, along with Facebook, Google, Microsoft, and Amazon, are Intel's so-called Super 7, customers so large and important that they get access to chips before the designs are released to other customers.[18] Data-center business accounts for over 30% of Intel's total revenue, and, according to the R&D leader, China probably accounts for 30% of that, second only to the United States. "Chinese internet companies' tech know-how still lags behind that of the US companies," the same R&D executive said. "So Intel has more influence on Alibaba and Tencent than on Google or Amazon. Future opportunities lie here."

Beyond the data-center business, Intel keeps investing in China. In 2014, it spent $1.5 billion to buy 20% of Tsinghua Unigroup, a state-affiliated company that owned China's top chip designers, Spreadtrum Communications and RDA Microelectronics. Intel also injected $100 million into Tsinghua University and Montage, a subsidiary of China's state-owned tech company, CEC, to form a joint venture on chip design. In 2018, after breaking up with Micron, its partner for developing nonvolatile memory chips, Intel partnered with Tsinghua Unigroup, providing memory chips for products like microSD cards and solid-state drives. And China remains the world's largest PC market, continuing to generate a big chunk of revenue for Intel.

Whether its success can continue is, of course, to be determined. Tan, for his part, isn't sure. "Nobody can dominate a market forever," he said. "Intel has done that for a long time. I do believe ultimately the Chinese challenge would come up somewhere along the line. It's just a matter of time."

Applying the Framework

Intel was one of the earliest Western companies to venture into China and has realized significant success by any measure. These factors were critical to the outcome:

- Over a multidecade period of increasing demand for computing, Intel brought a powerful alpha asset—a unique technology. Unlike with most other critical foreign technologies, the Chinese government and Chinese customers who wanted access to the best microprocessors had only one source: Intel. In fact, Intel long enjoyed the envied status of being able to "allocate" its sales, meaning it decided which customers to sell its microprocessors to. Inseparable from its superior chip design was Intel's market-leading manufacturing. Having a necessary, coveted, and impossible-to-replicate product is the ultimate alpha asset.
- The Chinese government understood that, in the coming decades, a vital semiconductor industry would be essential to its economy. Because of its de facto monopoly in high-performance microprocessors, Intel could enter China with little government interference or competition. This was not true for the similarly important automotive industry, where many foreign firms entered and the government could require joint ventures. Yet Intel did not exploit the power of its initial position. Instead, it embarked on building a now four-decade-long relationship with the Chinese government, aligning its business with China's national priorities.

Table 8.1: Summary of Success Factors for Intel

Factor		Explanation
Demand	▲▲▲	The computing revolution occurred in China, as in the rest of the world, fueling strong demand for microprocessors.
Access to market	▲	The Chinese government provided unfettered access to its markets on account of Intel's willingness to align with national priorities.
Advantage	▲▲▲	Intel's chips and production processes provided a wide moat, but Intel bolstered its competitive advantage by building its brand in China.
Commitment	▲▲	Intel has demonstrated a strong commitment to China, born from Andy Grove's vision. As a pioneer, the company endured many unprofitable years, yet it kept investing as China grew into the world's largest semiconductor consumer.
Governance	▲	Intel China was tightly integrated with headquarters because the technical requirements are too rarefied and the cost of fabs too great to have more than one global hub.
Leadership		Intel's local leadership showed savvy about China's politics and regulations as well as the diplomatic skills to succeed in a large, complex corporation. Both Wee Theng Tan and Ian Yang had influence in California. Tan enjoyed Grove's and other top managers' support, and Yang had Otellini's ear, later rising to be a member of Intel's executive management team.
Strategy	▲	Intel brought to China unparalleled technology, aligned its expansion plans with the government's national agenda, and built up its local brand.
Product		The technical complexity of the product and its manufacture does not allow for significant localization. However, the technical requirements for microprocessors are relatively uniform globally.
Agility		Intel proved that if local leaders are sufficiently skilled and persistent, a company can be agile even with global coordination. Tan reported to the general counsel, but he had a second reporting line to CEO Paul Otellini, whose influence he leveraged when needed.
Luck	▲	Intel was propelled by a multidecade megatrend favoring computing technology.

Note: Upward-pointing triangles indicate a positive factor. Downward-pointing triangles indicate a negative factor. The number of triangles is our subjective assessment of the relative importance of the factor. We omit indicators for those factors that we do not believe were significant for this case.

These elements and other factors in the framework are noted in Table 8.1, along with our subjective assessment of the decisive factors.

We now turn to the entirely different success story of Ermenegildo Zegna, a brand born in the Italian Alps more than a century ago.

Chapter 9

Zegna
When Brand Is King

Gildo Zegna, CEO of Ermenegildo Zegna, the luxury menswear brand, recalled how his family's business entered China in 1991. Few at the time would have predicted that one of the world's poorest countries would someday soon become the world's largest luxury market. "I must give credit to my father," he said. "He truly was the one who thought China would be a major force."[1]

Ermenegildo Zegna had founded his clothing company in 1910 in Trivero, a village in the foothills of the Italian Alps. His sons and their sons made a decision to venture to China. "Around the table, we decided to move on it," said Paolo Zegna, chairman of Ermenegildo Zegna.[2]

For Paolo, that was the charm of a family business—had Zegna not been family owned, it wouldn't have been able to go to China so early. "The stock market would not have understood it and would not have thought that could be the right thing to do," he said. But with only relatives as shareholders, "you can have a long-term vision and make decisions for what you believe they can bring back to the company."[3]

The return has been remarkable. Zegna now operates over 70 stores in China, from Sanya, in the far south, to Urumuqi, in the far northwest at the edge of the vast Taklamakan Desert. The Greater China region makes up a third of the company's revenue—€1.21 billion (about $1.42 billion) in 2018. Many other luxury brands have followed Zegna into China, but Zegna remains one of the most profitable.

Zegna's early entry is often cited as the reason for its success. In reality, that was just a small part of the story.

Who Can Afford It?

Zegna's first Chinese boutique was located in the Palace Hotel in Beijing, China's first luxury hotel. The spot was originally leased by Louis Vuitton. Yet amid political turmoil in 1989, Vuitton withdrew. Hiroshi Ogawa, a Japanese executive who led Zegna's entry, called his boss to discuss whether to leave too. The boss's response emboldened him: "We are not going to deal with the Chinese government. We are going to deal with the Chinese consumer."[4] Zegna opened its first store in 1991, as planned, in the location vacated by Vuitton.

In the early 1990s, Zegna's challenge was to find customers who could afford its pricey clothing—its suits sold for more than 10,000 RMB ($1,878) each. The average annual income for a Beijing resident was then about 3,500 RMB ($656). As a result, only the capitalist vanguard could shop at Zegna.

"The typical buyer was Rich Uncle," said Annie Hou, vice president of strategy at Ogilvy, a marketing agency.[5] "Rich Uncle" refers to a middle-aged Chinese man who seized on China's early economic reforms and made a fortune by running a private business. An Italian suit let him flaunt his gains.

Wenbin Wu was one. Born in the 1950s in an inland city, he moved to the coastal Guangdong province and opened a garment factory to contract orders from Hong Kong. By the mid-1990s, he'd made a fortune and enjoyed showing it off. He carried a brick-sized Motorola cell phone, drove a Mercedes-Benz, and dressed in Zegna. "In our circle, Zegna was well known," he said. "People recognized it when I entered the room. They knew I was rich, and that helped build my credential to do business with them."[6] Wu bought Zegna suits not only for himself but also for others who had the power to make or break his business deals, including government officials.

But the newly rich, like Wu, formed only a tiny fraction of China's over 1 billion people. From 1991 through 1996, Zegna endured five years of operating losses.[7] That didn't change the family's belief that a promising future lay ahead. At least, they were establishing their brand among China's elite. Before Zegna, the only luxury brands in China were Pierre Cardin and Montagut. Cardin made a name through a stunning women's fashion show, and Montagut through its polo shirts. Zegna offered the only formal menswear, allowing the company to entrench itself as the iconic suit brand, representing business success for Chinese consumers.

That competitive landscape soon changed. As in other markets, China's potential attracted a crowd. A wave of luxury brands entered in the 1990s, including Louis Vuitton, which returned in 1992. It was followed by Hermès, Gucci, Burberry, and Dior. After 2000, more flooded in. Zegna managed to maintain a strong position, owing to its reputation for product quality.

Quality, Service, and Talent

The company is vertically integrated. It has its own buyers, who purchase raw materials from Australia or China. It manufactures clothing in its factories across Europe and the United States and distributes through its stores around the world. This "sheep to shop" process is designed to ensure quality. The approach harks back to the Zegna family's roots. Ermenegildo started the company as a textile producer. It didn't launch its ready-to-wear men's line until the 1960s—half a century later. Even into the 2000s, Zegna still manufactured clothing for Gucci and Versace.

For years, fabric innovation had been the company's calling card. Members of the family traveled to Australia in the 1960s, looking for raw materials, and awarded Zegna trophies to producers of the finest wool. The company clings to that tradition. It has developed lightweight wools and wrinkle-free and stain-resistant fabrics. Heritage and craftsmanship are part of its pitch.

Yet a high-quality product wasn't enough to win in China; local tailors could offer a well-cut suit. Zegna strived to differentiate itself with its customer service. Gildo Zegna, the CEO and a member of the third generation of the family in the business, started his career in the United States as an assistant buyer for Bloomingdale's. There, he learned the value of developing client relationships and conceived a customer service approach for his family's company. "'After-sales service' is an American word, but we do that with our personal service," he said. "We keep notes on every customer, so that we always have their measurements and preferences for ready reference."[8]

That concept was implemented in China by Vittorio Proietti Tocca, Zegna's in-country retail director. He'd ventured to Asia in the 1990s, working for Zegna in Southeast Asia before alighting in China. He'd started his career as a sales associate and was known as a coddler of customers. He introduced to Zegna the concept of "clienteling," a fancy name for the simple idea that a company should build long-term relationships with customers by tracking their purchases and preferences. A former Zegna boutique manager, who was recruited from the hospitality industry, was given a book when he arrived at Zegna by Tocca, *Hug Your Customers*, by Jack Mitchell, chairman of Mitchell Stores, a US clothing retailer. "That was our bible," he said.[9] He had spent 14 years with Zegna and had experienced the company's rise in China firsthand.

By almost all accounts, Zegna was a leader in customer relationship management at the time. "When other luxury brands were taking customer information with paper and pen, we already used a computer-based system to manage all the data," the same manager said. A key performance indicator (KPI) of Zegna's stores was whether each customer was registered; that was linked to store employees' annual bonuses. "Our KPI must reach 90%. It sounds so simple, but that's the foundation of the customer management."

The customer profile includes name, age, profession, preferences, purchasing history, spending power, and other details. When Zegna held a marketing event, it would pull data based on various criteria and target customers who were most likely to purchase.

Zegna offered a variety of services to increase customer satisfaction, such as 30-day free returns versus the industry standard of 7 days. And it provided door-to-door service. Zegna's staffers would go to customers' homes to take measurements and then deliver a suit in a few weeks.

Zegna entered China when the luxury clothing market barely existed and no locals had experience with the distribution or merchandising of luxury goods. As a result, it brought managers from Italy and other developed countries. They would then train and develop the Chinese staff, equipping them with the skills to meet the demands of customers who could afford to buy a suit that could cost as much as a used car. For years, Zegna was considered a "luxury academy," and it trained a number of the members of the first generation of Chinese luxury professionals. Ken Kress, Zegna Asia Pacific president, once said: "We never cut the training budget, even amid an economic crisis."[10]

Zegna also provided opportunities for employees to advance. They could choose to be a specialist luxury consultant or a manager. Each year, the company sent a group of high-potential Chinese employees to New York and Milan for training.[11]

The Golden Era

With commerce flourishing in China, a relaxation of the country's investment strictures on foreign companies further fueled Zegna's growth. Before 2005, luxury brands entered China primarily through partnerships with local franchises or distributors. At the end of 2004, to meet obligations to the WTO, China removed this restriction, resulting in luxury brands reclaiming their sales rights. Zegna was one of the first to do so.

To gain access to the Chinese market, Zegna had operated its stores as partnerships with Chinese distributors. Starting in 2005, Zegna began to terminate these partnerships and open its own stores across the country and enlarge stores at premier locations. Zegna brought new products from its sportswear and leisurewear lines. And it adopted a decentralized buying model—a different approach from other luxury brands; retail managers could select products that were specific to individual stores.

"If the city was a more casual culture, they bought more casual collections," said Sally Stiegler, former Zegna Asia Pacific chief strategy officer. "If it was more of an office market, like Beijing, they bought more suits."[12] Zegna also became one of the first luxury brands to expand into China's lower-tier cities, where there was less competition and untapped demand. The China team led the effort. "They decided where to open the stores," said a former executive who had witnessed the company's expansion. "Back then, they had a lot of autonomy. Once the budget for China was finalized, they just went on to implement their plan. They really didn't have to always ask for permission from headquarters."[13] Stiegler echoed those remarks: "Mr. Zegna had great trust in the China leadership team," which then consisted of half Chinese and half foreigners with experience in Asia.

By 2008, Zegna owned all of its China stores. It could thus better manage its products, brand, and customer service. As a result, from 2006 through 2010, Zegna posted 30% of average annual sales growth in China.[14] In 2010, it was one of the top five brands, which together accounted for 50% of the sales of luxury menswear in the country.[15]

As Chinese consumers became increasingly important contributors to the company's revenue, Zegna began to tailor products to them. This started as early as 2005, when the company discovered that Chinese customers liked leather goods, so it developed accessories such as wallets and bags, which sold quite well. In 2008, the year Beijing hosted the Olympic Games, Zegna experimented with Olympic-themed products, like sunglasses. Again, those products were popular. One of the most successful items Zegna ever offered was a standing-collar jacket, a simple, casual look that was especially favored by government officials, whose preferences were deeply impacted by Chinese president Xi Jinping. Once Xi became president in 2012, a jacket of this style became his signature. He wore it everywhere, from a trip to a primary school in Fujian province to an appearance at Central Television. The *New York Times* even published an article headlined "China's Leader Wears Many Hats, but Only One Jacket."[16] Xi's style was soon adopted by his followers. A photo from the Xinhua News Agency showed an exhibition at the national museum in 2012: Five out of seven members of the Politburo Standing Committee turned up in similar jackets. A separate article from the news agency said: "No need for ironing, neat, stain resistant, and with a common touch, this has made the jacket a favorite informal attire for Chinese officialdom."[17] Zegna was the rare fashion house to benefit from a trend created by politicians, not a group known for being fashion forward.

Zegna would sell its China-developed products globally but usually launched them in China before expanding into other regions. But Zegna's China experiments weren't always successful. Its designers were based in Europe and lacked a nuanced understanding of the Chinese culture; sometimes their attempts at creativity went awry. The former boutique manager remembered the day he opened a box of new products from Europe and was appalled to see a shirt with the Chinese character "寿" embroidered on it. "That amounted to cursing people to die!" he said. "寿" means longevity in Chinese, but only the dead, before being buried or cremated, wear clothes with the character embroidered on them. Zegna ended up withdrawing the collection. Yet that incident didn't stop the efforts to cater to Chinese tastes. The company offered Chinese Zodiac-related products and shorter versions of its suits to fit Chinese sizes. Today, about one-fifth of Zegna's products in China are tailored specifically for Asian customers.

The Millennial Challenge

As China prospered, more of its younger generation became luxury customers. These people were born as China chugged toward becoming an economic power. As the only children in their families, due to China's one-child policy, they often enjoyed allowances from their parents. The *2017 China Luxury Market Study* by Bain showed that Chinese millennials had been major contributors to the growth of the country's luxury sector: They typically start purchasing at an earlier age and bought more frequently.[18]

Unlike their parents, who favor more formal attire, the younger Chinese generation, like their peers in the developed world, prefer a casual look—so-called streetwear or sportswear. Many of them have traveled overseas and shopped at boutiques in New York, Paris, Milan, and Tokyo. They're knowledgeable about fashion and zealous in their use of social media. According to research conducted by Ogilvy China in 2019, even a post-1990s consumer in China's less affluent, lesser known cities knows the names of 30 luxury brands.[19]

Though Zegna had developed leisurewear in the past, it mainly styled its clothing for business settings. To broaden its appeal, the company brought back Alessandro Sartori, who headed Z Zegna, a younger and more fashion-oriented line, from 2003 through 2011. At the end of 2017, Sartori launched Zegna Couture XXX, a tailoring-meets-sportswear collection, comprising T-shirts, sweatpants, polo shirts, blazers, outerwear, and sneakers. Carrying on the tradition of fabric innovation, the collection used materials Zegna hadn't used before, including machine-washable wool and technical silk. In China, the company recruited Hong Kong actor William Chan and Korean rapper Sehun Oh as the millennial faces of XXX and threw a three-day launch party in Shanghai. Five hundred attendees could use their WeChat IDs to unlock a variety of games and experiences, such as creating digital graffiti, making music videos, and getting personalized recommendations on XXX collections. Zegna was one of the first luxury brands to use WeChat in its merchandising. In 2017, Zegna offered 60 pairs of limited-edition Tiziano rainbow sneakers on WeChat, and those sold out within a few minutes.

The following year, Zegna extended its China-centered online marketing by opening a pop-up store on JD.com, one of the country's leading ecommerce platforms. In 2019, it launched another virtual store on Tmall Luxury Pavilion, Alibaba's premium brand site. One reason Zegna energetically chased this new, younger pool of potential customers was that its original pool was shrinking. An anticorruption campaign, pushed by Xi Jinping, had damped luxury demand. Zegna was one of the brands hardest hit, as a significant portion of its revenue came from "gifts." "Starting from 2014, there was a sharp drop in sales," said the former boutique manager. Sales in China fell 5% that year, and the *Financial Times* called it a nightmare year in emerging markets for Zegna.[20]

Despite all its efforts, Zegna's main Chinese customers have remained professionals in their mid-30s and beyond. People in their 20s mostly aren't interested. Zizhong Du, a 25-year-old graduate student, explained why. He's one of the *fuerdai*—the second-generation rich—and comes from Chengdu, a southwestern city. Growing up, he remembered seeing his father, a real estate developer, armored in Zegna for meetings and business dinners. "Zegna is my father's clothes," said Du. "I don't want to wear his clothes. I'm not that old."[21] His preferred brands included Gucci, Prada, Armani, and Louis Vuitton. One of his favorite fashion pieces was a Gucci jacket, with "Guccy" stitched on the back. That misspelling isn't a mistake but a playful mocking of fakes. "That's hilarious," he said. Coming from a country where fashion knockoffs have proliferated, the Guccy collection garnered attention. Du wore his jacket to a friend's party, and the attendees "all thought I'm cool."

In contrast to Zegna, Gucci has made progress in terms of winning over millennials. In 2018, 62% of its more than $8 billion in sales came from people under 35 years old. And by 2019, its fastest-growing segment was Generation Z, who then topped out at age 24.[22] Another brand that has become sought after among millennials is Louis Vuitton. A UBS report in 2018 estimated a third of Louis Vuitton's sales had come from millennials.[23]

Zegna has so far not been able to achieve that kind of cachet among younger Chinese buyers. "Zegna being formal wear for middle-aged successful men is too ingrained," said the former Zegna China executive. "With athleisure becoming a new trend, some other luxury brands also face similar challenges. All of a sudden, everybody is wearing sneakers."

Keep Moving Forward

Zegna hasn't given up on updating its image. In August 2018, the company announced it would buy an 85% stake in Thom Browne, a trendsetting fashion brand based in New York. Thom Browne had 31 stores worldwide, and Zegna planned to open an additional 10 in China and Japan. That deal not only refreshed Zegna's brand but also expanded its physical presence. The company now has around 72 stores across China, more than Gucci's 50 and Louis Vuitton's 45. This has the potential to be a competitive advantage. According to McKinsey's *China Luxury Report 2019*, 92% of luxury purchases were made off-line.[24] "There is a trust issue," said Ogilvy's Hou. "People are still afraid of getting counterfeits online."

In addition, though online outreach can educate and influence consumers, McKinsey found that in-person experiences mattered most when it came time to purchase for 9 out of 10 young Chinese consumers. Zegna has such a presence in nearly each of China's 23 provinces and 4 municipalities.

As the COVID-19 pandemic took hold in China, Zegna closed stores whose locations were hardest hit by the pandemic and reduced operating hours of those remaining open. As the virus became more contained, by early April even stores in Wuhan, the epicenter, had reopened. In July, Zegna launched a new store in Chengdu, a southwestern metropolis.

Though the luxury industry took a massive hit worldwide, the Chinese market rebounded quickly. Several brands reported an uptick in China—Tiffany's retail sales surged around 30% in April and 90% in May compared with the same months from the previous year. Burberry announced in May that sales of its clothing, bags, and accessories in China were "already ahead of the prior year."[25] And a Hermès boutique took in $2.7 million on its reopening day.[26] "Leading luxury brands in China all saw double-digital growth," said a luxury practitioner. "Zegna probably has also benefited from the trend." The surge in sales, according to the practitioner, was mainly attributed to a shift from overseas shopping to local shopping. Chinese consumers usually make more than half of luxury purchases abroad. Yet COVID-19 keeps them from traveling and traps spending at home.

With the Browne purchase, Zegna announced to young Chinese (and the world) that it's no longer the company that dresses dad for business meetings. But a brand like Zegna's is also a promise to its longtime customers that whatever they value in it will endure. For Zegna, even as it repositions itself, that promise remains rooted in its heritage of delivering the finest fabrics.

Applying the Framework

The Greater China region makes up a third of Zegna's revenue, and the company is one of the most profitable luxury brands in China. These factors were critical to its success:

- China's GDP grew from 1979 through 1989 at a rate of 8.6% per year. That rapid growth resulted in a cadre of rich Chinese, most of them male. They wanted to purchase better goods and signal their success. Zegna bet this growth would continue and would create significant demand for luxury menswear. It bet correctly.
- Zegna brought several alpha assets to China. First was its famous brand. A local rival could not create a brand with the European heritage of Zegna; Italian menswear is prized by the fashion conscious worldwide. Zegna's product quality also set it apart. The company is vertically integrated and oversees each stage of its production, from fabric purchasing to design and manufacturing, which ensures delivery of the high-quality products the brand promises. Zegna's culture of customer engagement was also unique in China. It employed managers with long tenures, who could inculcate its values in a subsidiary far from headquarters in the Italian foothills.
- Luck favored Zegna repeatedly. Few people in the late 1980s predicted how quickly the Chinese luxury market would develop. Of course, the market could have gone the opposite way, especially after the political turmoil.

Table 9.1: Summary of Success Factors for Zegna

Factor		Explanation
Demand	▲▲	The luxury market expanded dramatically along with China's prosperity more generally.
Access to market		Because of government restrictions, Zegna formed partnerships with Chinese distributors at first. When restrictions were lifted, Zegna reclaimed its distribution and streamlined management of its brand, products, and services, which resulted in rapid growth.
Advantage	▲	Zegna offered a genuine European heritage, impossible for a local rival to replicate. Its products offered superior quality, and its customer focus was distinctive.
Commitment	▲	Zegna's origins in Italy may have contributed to its willingness to commit to China. Italy is a small market. For Zegna to keep growing, it had to go global. For an American company, global markets are nice to have. For an ambitious Italian company, they're imperative. Yet, for the luxury retail sector, an initial commitment can be small, followed by further commitment with further success.
Governance		Zegna's governance structure followed the typical multinational's China model, with the China executive reporting to the Asia Pacific president.
Leadership		The local leadership, due to the lack of a luxury segment in China until recently, has not included mainland Chinese. Given that the development of company culture was a lodestar in the early days, selecting executives with experience with Zegna made sense.
Strategy	▲▲	Start small, build the brand, focus on the customer, and invest further with proven success. This strategy makes sense for a family business with a long planning horizon.
Product		Limited localization for the Chinese consumer. Part of the appeal of the brand is its European heritage.
Agility		Zegna's choices for governance and local leadership did not maximize agility. Relative to some of the other markets discussed in this book, agility may be less critical in luxury retail. The China team did enjoy some autonomy during the rapid growth years, with authority to make most decisions within their overall budget constraints.
Luck	▲	Lucky breaks included the Chinese government allowing wholly owned subsidiaries of luxury brands to operate in China and riding the wave of Xi Jinping–style clothing.

Note: Upward-pointing triangles indicate a positive factor. Downward-pointing triangles indicate a negative factor. The number of triangles is our subjective assessment of the relative importance of the factor. We omit indicators for those factors that we do not believe were significant for this case.

So Zegna's bet, though based on its vision, returned the lucky outcome. Then Zegna got a break when the Chinese government allowed wholly owned subsidiaries of luxury brands to operate in China. It also benefited from a trend created by Chinese president Xi Jinping. No one ever would've predicted a politician would become a fashion influencer.

These elements and other factors in the framework are noted in Table 9.1, along with our subjective assessment of the decisive factors.

By arriving in China early, Zegna positioned itself to profit when luck came its way. Today, the company does face challenges. Its products have been favored by the older generation in China, and the company is still working to win over younger Chinese men. As the former Zegna executive said: "It takes time to refresh a brand image." Indeed, the enduring image that makes a brand such a powerful alpha asset when it aligns with macro trends is exactly what makes it so hard to reposition when markets change.

Chapter 10

Lessons on Winning and Losing in China

In chapter 2, we argued that to succeed in China a company must satisfy the three necessary conditions and competently make five categories of managerial decisions, from which can emerge agility, also an important factor. We further recognized that luck can help or hurt. Table 10.1 summarizes our assessment of the relative importance of each factor on the outcomes we observed in the eight case studies.

Demand

The key question for a foreign firm entering a new market is whether potential customers need the goods and services the firm has the alpha assets to deliver with a competitive advantage. For Amazon, Norwegian Cruise Line, Hyundai, Intel, and InMobi, demand was evident from the outset. Demand then strengthened with time for Amazon, Hyundai, and Intel. Sequoia bet that demand for venture capital would grow in China. It was right, and booming demand fueled its success. Zegna also bet correctly that demand for its clothing would rise with China's GDP. For LinkedIn, lack of demand was an impediment. Chinese professionals wanted to advance their careers, but LinkedIn learned they did not want to display their profiles online and construct business-only online networks, as with its offering elsewhere. LinkedIn improvised with Chitu. However, for this pursuit, it lacked alpha assets.

Table 10.1: Summary of Success Factors for All Eight Cases

	Amazon	NCL	Hyundai I	Hyundai II	LinkedIn	Sequoia	InMobi	Intel	Zegna
Necessary conditions									
Demand	▲▲▲	▲	▲▲	▲▲	▽	▲▲▲	▲▲	▲▲▲	▲▲
Access		▲						▲	
Advantage		▽	▲▲▲	▲	▽	▲▲▲	▲	▲▲▲	▲
Managerial decisions									
Commitment	▽	▽▽▽	▲▲▲	▲▲▲	▲	▲▲▲	▲▲▲	▲▲	▲
Governance	▽	▽	▽	▽		▲▲▲	▲▲▲	▲	
Leadership	▽				▽				
Strategy	▽	▽	▲▲	▽	▽▽▽		▲	▲	▲▲
Product	▽	▽▽		▽	▽		▲		
Agility	▽▽				▽▽	▲▲▲	▲▲		
Luck	▽			▽▽▽		▲	▲	▲	▲

Note: Upward-pointing triangles indicate a positive factor. Downward-pointing triangles indicate a negative factor. The number of triangles is our subjective assessment of the relative importance of the factor. We omit indicators for those factors that we do not believe were significant for these cases.

Access to the Market

Our sample is necessarily selected from firms that did manage to enter China, but in our view, government regulation is a make-or-break factor for only a very few industries, such as higher education, telecommunications, military, and media. Intel and Norwegian Cruise Line were encouraged to enter the market by the Chinese government, although the importance of the semiconductor industry required that Intel invest significant managerial attention in building and sustaining strong political relationships. Hyundai had no alternative but to form a joint venture with a Chinese company. Zegna got lucky when partnership requirements were relaxed after it entered. For Sequoia, LinkedIn, Amazon, and InMobi, access to the market required navigating some regulations, but that did not determine their fortunes.

Advantage and Alpha Assets

Just one of the companies we featured, Intel, brought overwhelming alpha assets to China. Its chip technology is the ultimate alpha asset—Intel had a virtual monopoly on the central processing unit that powered the PC revolution. Hyundai probably had the next strongest position, possessing a nearly unique capability to produce automobiles at low cost during a period of growing demand. Sequoia's brand gave it a head start among Chinese entrepreneurs. Zegna's alpha assets were brand and culture, helpful but perhaps not decisive. InMobi possessed a good-enough mobile advertising solution when few others were in the market. It knew this source of advantage was fleeting, and so it scrambled like a start-up to build a more sustainable advantage by bringing many users onto its platform. Neither Norwegian Cruise Line nor Amazon brought powerful brands, scale economies, or unique offerings to China, especially in the face of intense competition. In the West, LinkedIn's alpha asset was its customer network, but that failed to attract Chinese professionals,

beyond the relatively small group who worked for foreign multinationals or aimed to.

Commitment

All of our success stories eventually involved large commitments, but
the full commitment was rarely required from the outset. Zegna
started with a single store and a partner, although it did persist
patiently in experimenting with and developing the Chinese market
over decades. Sequoia raised a first fund and hired a partner and,
after its early successes, increased its commitment. For InMobi, Intel,
and LinkedIn, the initial investments did not require betting the
company, but the commitments were certainly meaningful expen-
ditures for the parent. InMobi and Intel doubled down as their odds
improved. LinkedIn scaled back when its initial strategy faltered.
Hyundai, in contrast, had to make a large multiyear bet on an assembly plant and distribution network before it could sell its first car.

For Norwegian Cruise Line, the commitment to build a new ship
for the Chinese market was huge, but it turned out that the ship was
redeployable to Alaska with some refurbishment. NCL quit after its
first attempt did not show promising results. Amazon had to invest
significantly to establish a presence, but the stakes kept rising as well-
funded competitors bet huge sums to acquire a dominant position.
At that point, as huge opportunity costs arose, it retreated. Although
in the larger context, NCL and Amazon perhaps made the best available use of shareholder capital by quitting, with their retreats clearly
ending their prospects in China.

Governance, Leadership, and Agility

Probably the most consistent lesson from our research is that agility
arising from autonomy in governance and leadership prefigures success. This is nerve-racking for executives of a parent company—they
understandably will not want to relinquish control but must realize
that excessive oversight leads to sluggishness in China. For Amazon,

its alpha assets were insufficient to overcome its lack of agility. Contrast that with InMobi, which granted nearly full autonomy to its China head, essentially launching a start-up that beat speedy local rivals.

Still, even for governance, one size does not fit all. A fully autonomous Intel China makes no sense, given the resources required to develop and manufacture chips. And, given that Zegna's key alpha asset was its heritage and culture of customer care, it had to tightly integrate its China team with the rest of the company. Its aim was to translate that culture in China, and it managed to do so.

The successful leaders in our cases come from many backgrounds. Sequoia and InMobi were launched in China by Western-educated mainland Chinese. Zegna and Intel were not. Those companies tapped managers with experience with the parent company. Sequoia and InMobi bet on outsiders. For most companies, an ideal China leader cannot be found, if he or she even exists. Most companies will have to choose a leader with either deep experience in China or strong ties to headquarters and hope that this person can compensate for any deficiencies.

Strategy

Strategy formulation from the outset is good discipline, requiring that the management team consider whether its initial plan calls on the company's alpha assets and is realistic about committed resources. Most of our cases describe sensible initial strategies. Amazon brought its "one best way" to China, as it had to other global markets. LinkedIn planned to connect Chinese professionals in the way it had their counterparts in the United States and Europe. Hyundai aimed to use its scale and its tightly integrated supplier network to deliver an affordable car to the Chinese middle class. The weakness for these companies was in not modifying their strategies when early results suggested difficulties. Zegna improvised when regulations allowed greater independence. InMobi did so when it realized the Chinese market was too different to allow its global solution to prevail. For

Hyundai an initially successful strategy was not followed by a modification of its plans to adapt to a changing market and more intense competition.

Product

All of the companies we studied adapted their products for Chinese customers. The critical decision each company made was in determining its *platform boundary*—which elements of the global offering were standard and which could be localized. The location of the boundary depends on two drivers. First, how different are the customer needs in China? Second, how much cost and effort will localization require? For Intel, its microprocessors must be standard globally. For Amazon, the Chinese consumer differed enough that more localization was needed. Of course, getting the product just right, even given a willingness to adapt, is tricky. Norwegian Cruise Line showed great willingness to localize, but missed the mark, and retooling a cruise ship is not as easy as modifying the user interface on a mobile app.

Luck

A lot of books about business offer simple formulas. And humans do like simple causal explanations for almost everything from child rearing to happiness. When we started this project, the coronavirus was still confined to bats, and there were a dozen flights per day between San Francisco and China. As we were writing, we coauthors were quarantined on two different continents. Luck, or randomness, if that label makes you feel less helpless, remains a hugely important factor in business as in life—and especially so when a business involves geopolitics, the macroeconomy, technological change, and the dynamics of the natural world. In every one of our cases, luck mattered. Hyundai faced decisively bad luck with geopolitics when the United States deployed its missile defense system in South Korea. Amazon encountered surprisingly fierce competition. All four of our success stories included good fortune. Luck cannot be controlled, but the best managers can at least be ready to confront randomness by imagining scenarios, drafting contingency plans, and being prepared to respond to whatever the future brings.

Revisiting the Default Hypotheses

We opened the book by listing the default hypotheses that even casual observers would cite to explain business success in China, including the role of government, differences in Chinese consumers' tastes, and cultural challenges. All of these hypotheses are supported to some extent by the experiences of the companies we studied and are reflected in our framework. The role of government falls within our necessary condition of access to the market. Differences in consumer preferences are subsumed by adaptation of the offering to the market. Cultural variation in management styles is addressed within our factors of leadership and governance. However, the initially hypothesized factor of guanxi—or China's particular reliance on informal influence networks—appears, at least in our cases, to be less important than we had expected. Trust and personal relationships remain critical in doing business in China but not more so than elsewhere. Chinese business today seems to us very much no-nonsense. You may get an introduction to a business contact because of guanxi, but we haven't learned of many irrational deals done to satisfy the demands of social allegiance. Even the style of business seems to have evolved. In the early 2000s, doing business over long 12-course dinners with a lot of baijiu toasts was common. Not today. In fact, we've recently observed managers and entrepreneurs doing two successive one-hour dinners in one evening for two different business matters.

Chapter 11

Prescriptions for Success

At the beginning of this book, we defined success as meeting a significant share of demand in a market category with sustained competitive advantage. Achieve that, and financial returns will follow. Four of our eight cases tracked China successes. While our sample is not random, we do *not* believe the chance of success for the average company entering China is greater than 50%. But as with anything, you can raise those odds if you take time to reflect and plan. In this chapter, we provide specific advice for how to assess the chances of success for your company and increase your chances of success. Throughout this book, we have emphasized that luck matters, and we're not now backing away from that. There is no fail-safe for success in China. But the most common pitfalls can be avoided by learning from the experiences of others.

Our process for assessing your chances of success and avoiding mistakes flows from our framework for understanding the successes and failures of the companies we examined. From the three necessary conditions—demand, access to the market, and alpha assets—one can assess whether entering China should even be considered. Then, from the five managerial decisions, you can extract lessons from our case studies about approaches that have worked and on which idiosyncratic conditions those approaches have depended.

Assessing the Opportunity

All the cases here have played out sufficiently that they can be examined retrospectively. Managers contemplating entering China face a harder challenge: predicting the likelihood of success. Companies aim to invest where they're likely to see the best financial returns. China is one opportunity—a potentially immense one—but it must vie for resources with others within the company, including creating products and services for existing markets or entering adjacent markets in regions where you're already thriving.

Imagine a hypothetical company, Ping Technologies, which has succeeded in the United States and Europe with augmented-reality (AR) exercise equipment. A treadmill, stair climber, or stationary bike is used at home with an AR environment created on a large screen in front of the exerciser. Ping immerses the user in a natural environment—maybe Machu Picchu in Peru or Half Dome at Yosemite National Park—using only a conventional high-definition flat display. Ping has discovered that social interaction with other participants from all over the world increases how much people exercise. Friendships, business deals, and romances have developed on account of Ping, often across cultures. Ping is no stranger to China, having developed its equipment with a Chinese manufacturer in Shenzhen. Recently, Ping has noticed growing demand from Chinese customers, even though Ping has no market presence in China and customers there must buy through gray-market intermediaries at high cost and use an English-language version of the product. Ping is considering launching a new venture to exploit this perceived opportunity.

In assessing whether the opportunity is real, the first question is the extent of the demand for Ping in China. One way to approach the assessment of demand is to use the *abstraction ladder* technique, inspired by the famous quote by Theodore Levitt, a former professor at Harvard Business School. Levitt's adage: "Customers don't want to buy a quarter-inch drill. They want a quarter-inch hole."[1] To use this technique, Ping should state the job it does in its home market—

for instance, "We help people exercise at home while exploring the world with like-minded friends." Ping then would consider why a customer wants it to do this job—the more abstract motive for wanting to accomplish the task. For instance, the customer might buy the Ping system to "make exercise more fun." The abstraction ladder can be continued, resulting in ever more abstract jobs, such as "improve personal fitness" or even "increase life expectancy." When posed sufficiently abstractly (for example, to increase life expectancy), demand will almost certainly exist in China. However, if few Chinese consumers do aerobic exercise daily or if they have little space in their homes for a bulky piece of exercise gear, then the demand for Ping may not be as high as expected. This deliberate consideration of the job you do allows your firm to estimate the total market size but also to understand where Chinese culture and customs may deviate from those in your existing markets. This enables a realistic assessment of the fraction of a market you can reasonably address with your product or service.

If potential Chinese companies already do the job in exactly the same way it is done in the home market—say, by using Chinese-made AR exercise equipment—a company like Ping is unlikely to find customers. But if Ping's offering is distinct, the company may enjoy an opening. Ping then faces uncertainty about whether customers will flock to its AR bikes, treadmills, and stair climbers. The sweet spot for any company contemplating a China expansion is a growing market with limited local competition. Ping might conclude that China has a sizable, growing market for home exercise equipment and that the distinct benefits of its AR and social engagement provide its opening. Imagine that it then estimates the total addressable market to be "only" around 25 million households in China. That number, although only a small percentage of China's total, would still represent Ping's largest global market.

As a practical matter, to succeed in China, Ping must have access to the market, and it therefore needs to verify the legal means by which it can enter. Rarely would a sector not be served at all by some foreign firms, and so one way to assess feasibility is to catalog foreign competitors and learn their legal structures. Let's suppose Ping learned a US stationary-bike maker was using a wholly owned foreign entity (WOFE) to serve China. Ping would conclude it could likely enter without a partner. Ping could then assess regulatory constraints and legal structures with the help of a Chinese affiliate of its law firm. In most industries, either a WOFE or a joint venture is likely feasible.

Given sufficient demand and a legal charter to operate, Ping's success will depend critically on the possession of alpha assets. A straightforward approach to assessing potential advantages is to list the possible alpha assets in the domestic market along with an *alpha score*, calculated as the product of a 10-point assessment of the extent to which the asset is *rare* (i.e., difficult for rivals to acquire) and a 10-point assessment of the extent to which it's *necessary* to do the job (i.e., cannot be easily substituted with an alternative). Then estimate the alpha score for those same assets in the Chinese market. For example, a brand is usually a legal trademark, can't be acquired by rivals, and thus scores a 10 on rarity. However, if a brand is completely unknown in a new market, it cannot be necessary in that market. Any rival's brand is likely just as good and so the necessity score would be 0. The combined alpha score would be $10 \times 0 = 0$. An example of this analysis for a set of potential alpha assets is shown in Table 11.1.

Ping clearly faces some weaknesses. Chinese consumers are unaware of its brand, which is hot at home, and the company does not yet have a distribution network in China. Yet its AR technology is quite good and would likely take a rival at least two years to replicate. Further, its global customer network is potentially highly valuable, as one of Ping's main benefits for customers is connecting them with people all over the world. This creates *network effects* that are a significant barrier to competition.

Even if the estimated demand is real, an opportunity may not offer a sufficient financial return to make it attractive. Our four successful cases—Sequoia, Intel, Zegna, and InMobi—all enjoyed outcomes for which the economic value of the business in China had the potential to become a significant share of their profits.

Table 11.1: Assessment of Alpha Assets at Home and in China for the Ping Illustrative Example

Asset	Home market			China			Notes
	Rarity (R)	Necessity (N)	Alpha score (R × N)	Rarity (R)	Necessity (N)	Alpha score (R × N)	
Solution—AR exercise gear	8	8	64	8	8	64	For 2+ years, the technology will be hard to replicate. Unlikely someone will attempt this until market is proven.
Production scale economies	8	5	40	9	5	45	No large rival producers, so Ping has greatest scale. If successful, the market will be large enough for a domestic rival. Necessity is questionable—would not be too hard to find an efficient supplier.
"Ping" brand	10	6	60	10	0	0	The brand is little known in China. It can be an alpha asset in the future, but to realize this goal, brand building must be the focus of the China unit in the first two years.
Global customer network	10	8	80	10	5	50	The global customer network is a critical success factor and very hard to replicate once established. However, a key uncertainty is how valuable the global experience will be for the Chinese consumer.

Note: This table captures the management team's subjective assessment of the rarity and necessity of each alpha asset on a scale of 1 to 10, with the product of the two resulting in an *alpha score* of 1 to 100.

For Amazon and NCL, in contrast, huge opportunity costs rendered the prize not worth it.

In theory, a large company should have sufficient access to capital to pursue any opportunity that promises to return more than the opportunity cost of capital. However, a hurdle this low rarely exists in practice. A more critical constraint is often the capacity required to manage an expansion into a market as large and complex as China. The choice to enter China entails high opportunity costs, and a venture there must offer hefty financial returns to warrant a green light.

Three main factors drive the size of the financial return for any company: How big is the market? How much competitive advantage and therefore market share and profit margin can the company create? And what is the probability of actually realizing projections of revenues and profits, given execution risks (the known unknowns) and the role of randomness (unknown unknowns)?

Two techniques may help in evaluating a potential payoff. A *decision tree* can be used to incorporate binary outcomes into scenarios.[2] For example, a critical, binary question is whether Tencent would support the integration of Ping into WeChat, which has been essential to acquiring customers in China. Estimates for the probability of the outcomes like this can be used to risk adjust the financial scenarios.

In a second approach, *Monte Carlo simulations* can be used to estimate outcomes.[3] Uncertainties to incorporate may include the average sustainable subscription price, the fraction of the market that adopts Ping, and the customer acquisition cost. Assumptions about the range and uncertainty of these parameters can be combined in a financial simulation to characterize possible outcomes.

These techniques ensure that projections of the potential financial reward—which will be tempting to overestimate, given the immensity of China's economy—will be tempered by the odds that the venture won't deliver on its promise. For the opportunity to survive scrutiny, the eventual prize must be dazzling.

Preparing for Success

If the opportunity does dazzle, the focus turns to how to maximize the chances of realizing its potential. The steps required correspond to the five managerial decisions in our framework.

Commitment

Success in China is expensive. The main pitfall to be avoided is to launch a China venture with an unrealistic expectation of the cost and therefore squander resources in an effort that was doomed because of insufficient investment. Fortunately, the commitment need not be forever or unconditional. The questions to be answered before plunging ahead are: (a) What are the phases and decision points, (b) What's the cost of the first phase, and (c) How will the success of that phase be evaluated? The first phase is likely to require at least two years before the venture can be reasonably assessed. Of course, a pro forma plan should be prepared for three to five years, but that plan will require regular revision. The key discipline needed at this phase is avoiding self-delusion and verifying that budgeted resources are consistent with a realistic assessment of what's needed.

Could Ping make a two-year commitment to a pilot in Shanghai and Beijing and reasonably address the key uncertainties? Which questions should Ping tackle? A few jump to mind. Will Tencent allow Ping to be integrated into WeChat? What will it cost to acquire customers? What monthly subscription price will work? Will Chinese users want to engage with others globally? Will advertisers pay to appear on the platform?

Answering these questions does not demand building factories or rolling out a nationwide marketing campaign. Rather, doing so requires a consumer marketing team with local knowledge and experience, leasing and staffing two retail stores for demonstrating the exercise equipment, and funding a China team to localize the products' language and the Tencent integration features. Let's say Ping estimates the required investment will be $10 million per year for the first two years. A two-year commitment will then require Ping's management to allocate $20 million, at which point the long-term promise of the venture will likely be much clearer and financial projections more reliable.

Governance

Bain and Company has created a framework called RAPID to clarify decision-making roles in situations such as this one.[4] The five roles are *recommend*, provide *input*, *approve*, *decide*, and *perform*. The China unit will be responsible for performing and will recommend courses of action, but when does the China unit have the authority to approve and decide? Clearly some decisions cannot be made autonomously—Ping's name cannot be unilaterally changed to China AR Adventures. But can the China unit hire a celebrity athlete endorser without approval from headquarters? Can it change prices? We recommend that the launch team explicitly describe the categories of decisions that will likely be encountered, with specific examples of each, and document who will make the decision for each category. The lesson from our case studies is clear: The China unit must have substantial autonomy—likely even more than units in other locations.

Leadership

An effective leader in China is as rare as Ming dynasty porcelain. Cultural ambidexterity is valuable but so is organizational ambidexterity. The China leader must be both entrepreneur *and* corporate diplomat. Forced to choose, we feel the entrepreneurial side matters more, particularly in the first two or three years. A China unit is essentially a start-up, boosted by the parent's alpha assets. Betting on a leader recruited from the outside is of course riskier than promoting an insider. Taking a cue from Sequoia, we recommend creating "filaments" between home and China. The filaments will depend on the strengths and weaknesses of your people but may include recruiting deputies from the parent with deep expertise, investing in frequent travel between China and home, or having the China head spend a period at headquarters during the planning phase of the venture.

Agility

Smart governance and clear thinking give rise to agility. The closest thing we have to a prescription here is that, as with everything except alcohol and in-laws, more is always better. Domestic rivals will almost certainly include cat-quick start-ups. Even with powerful alpha assets, a foreign company entering China must plan to relax some of its governance rules to be agile. Yes, there are risks of missteps by an autonomous team, but the opportunity costs of sluggishness are greater. Don't be a sloth that gets overtaken by a cheetah.

Strategy

An initial strategy should follow from the state of the market and from the alpha assets of the company. For instance, Ping faces no domestic rival yet has a compelling technology; it has a large global customer network but lacks a strong brand in China. It expects its technology to give it a two- or three-year head start on a potential rival. A strategy might be stated as follows: "Launch among the business elite in Shanghai and Beijing, using demos in stores at luxury malls. Recruit a celebrity-athlete endorser and use key opinion leaders to build brand awareness and adoption in the upper middle class, as stores are expanded to other first-tier cities." In developing a strategy, the team should consider alternative approaches and vet them with a broad group of stakeholders. Once selected, the strategy must be clearly articulated. Mike Tyson's boxing adage applies here: "Everyone has a plan until they get punched in the mouth." The strategy will unquestionably evolve as it is tested against the market.

Product

All products for the Chinese market must be localized to some extent, even if merely in the language of the instruction manual. In most cases, more significant tailoring is required. The question to answer from the outset is, Which elements of the product are part of a global platform and which can be changed for China?[5] For Intel, global variation in chips is very limited, because creating fundamentally different versions is extraordinarily expensive and customer needs in a microprocessor don't vary with longitude. However, for InMobi, the entire mobile computing ecosystem varies significantly between China and its other markets, and creating more than one version of its software is not too expensive. As with our prescription for commitment levels, good discipline requires smart choices about localization: What will be standardized globally and what can vary? Who has the decision rights? Is the commitment of resources consistent with the expected level of product adaptation? For Ping, a key attraction of its system would be the global network of users, and so the AR software would have to be interoperable across all regions. Thus the core technology could be and should be standardized. Yet equipment sizing may need to be adjusted for smaller body statures and homes in China, and obviously the user interface must be in Chinese.

Luck

Random factors can be divided into those known and unknown unknowns. For the former, the best one can do is to list the uncertainties, scope out the range of possible outcomes, and consider actions needed under various scenarios to address them.

For instance, for Ping, if AR home exercise were to take off, the entry of a domestic imitator would be likely. What might be the strategy of that rival? How might Ping's initial choice of strategy and product depend on that eventuality? Does the business plan still work in the face of that competitive pressure? The specifics of the known unknowns are unpredictable, but their possible forms can be planned for.

The unk-unks by definition cannot be predicted, except to acknowledge that they will arise and complicate a China plan. One way to "plan" for them is to ensure that the China opportunity is attractive enough to surmount setbacks. This may be thought of as building in a margin of error. Beyond that, the unk-unks are one of the main reasons agility matters so much.

The Business Plan

As with any venture, a new China venture is merely a hypothesis that value can be created with an investment. Yet a firm can realistically assess its chances and, in doing so, decide whether the risk-adjusted return is worthwhile. This decision is necessarily supported by a business plan. That plan will inform debate within the firm. A suggested outline would read as follows:

- What job are we setting out to do in China?
  - For whom are we doing the job?
  - Who is now doing the job and how?
  - How large is demand, for the category as a whole and for our approach?
  - What is the likely growth rate of this market and of our approach?
- How will we navigate the legal constraints to access the market, and which legal form will we use?
  - With whom, if anyone, will we partner?
- What are our alpha assets in China? Will they sustain advantage?
  - Which alpha assets should we focus on building in the first year or two?

- What is our estimate of the risk-adjusted return for the China venture?
    - Is there enough margin of error to account for unk-unks?
- What commitment of resources is required?
    - What are the key milestones and which criteria will we use for deciding whether to continue with the venture?
- How will the China unit be organized and governed?
    - Which decisions require coordination with the home office?
    - How can we connect headquarters and the China unit?
- Who will lead the China unit?
    - What are the desirable characteristics of the leadership team?
    - Who are the candidates?
- What is our top-level strategy?
    - What are credible alternatives?
    - What are some possible competitive responses? How would we adapt to these?
- To what extent do we expect to adapt our offerings to the Chinese market?
    - How much will we standardize our offering?
    - Is our assumption about the extent of local customization realistic, given the commitment of resources, the governance structure, the strategy, and the leadership team?

Some companies should *not* attempt to enter China. Be clear-eyed and self-critical about the value of the opportunity, relative to other uses of your shareholders' capital and your managerial capacity. Then, as China's leader Deng Xiaoping famously said about the economic reforms that he led, "You must cross the river by feeling the stones with your feet."

Conclusion
Most Interesting Times

In the introduction, we argued that China was different enough that it deserved its own study. The cases we examine underscore the uniqueness of China. The vastness of the Chinese market and the availability of Chinese talent and capital guarantee that local competition will be tough. A local company will see, in any significant emerging need, the possibility of building a large and valuable business. Winning a market in China will be so lucrative (and prestigious) as to justify a do-or-die focus for Chinese entrepreneurs. This is true for perhaps no other emerging global market other than India. This characteristic of China underscores the criticality of properly assessing demand, making a sufficient commitment, setting up an agile governance structure, articulating a coherent strategy, and adapting the product or service to the market. Yet, a framework pressure tested for China should apply well to global expansion more generally. Entering Belgium also requires demand, access to the market, alpha assets, and so forth. We hope this book provides relevant lessons for any global manager.

Looking to the Future

Facing the prospect of a global slowdown amid the repercussions of COVID-19, the future for foreign companies in China may not look as promising as it once did. We predict the continued duality of laissez-faire and a visible government hand in the Chinese economy.

That's probably the most certain statement in this book. Some increase in tensions between China and the West seems unavoidable, but we cannot predict just how tense the 2020s will be. Chinese GDP will grow, making the country's markets even more attractive. Even as the pandemic disrupted the global economy, Walmart announced that it would invest 3 billion yuan ($425 million) in Wuhan, the original epicenter of the virus, over the next five years. Starbucks said that it would invest 900 million yuan ($130 million) to build a roasting plant in the eastern Chinese city of Kunshan.[1] In addition to its cities, China has a vast rural area with a population of 500 million people where few multinationals have ventured. Seeking high margins there probably won't work, given the lower purchasing power. Yet that huge population still offers ample opportunities to make profits. As long as companies know how to recognize demand and deploy their alpha assets to meet that demand, the return on investment may be as good as chasing the middle class.

Economic growth in China is now slowing, as was inevitable. As a result, efforts to grab market share in emerging categories will likely become less frenzied, and companies will eventually have to make profits. We predict this will require some rationalization of pricing and service levels in all sectors.

We also predict the emergence of strong Chinese brands and the development of other powerful alpha assets in Chinese companies. These companies are likely to be formidable competitors when they seek to expand from China to other global markets. That's already happened with such Chinese outfits as Lenovo and Huawei Technologies. Expect more like them.

"May you live in interesting times" is erroneously described as an ancient Chinese curse.[2] In reality, this "curse" can be traced back about a century ago to the British statesman Joseph Chamberlain. And he actually said, "I think that you will all agree that we are living in most interesting times. I never remember myself a time in which our history was so full, in which day by day brought us new objects of interest, and, let me say also, new objects for anxiety." Chamberlain's words are an apt summary of the situation for any businessperson considering an expansion into today's China.

Acknowledgments

When people were willing to speak with us with attribution, we identify them when we quote them. We thank them all for their willingness to share their stories and insights. Discussion of failure can be sensitive. Many thoughtful managers spoke to us on conditions of anonymity, and so we do not acknowledge them by name. Nevertheless, we thank them all for their candor and for their willingness to share their experiences for the benefit of others. Rui Ma and Sissi Zuo read the manuscript carefully and provided helpful suggestions for improvement.

We are grateful for the financial support of the Wharton School Global Initiatives Research Fund, without which this book would not have been possible.

Tim Gray skillfully and swiftly edited the entire book, merging our styles and improving our prose.

We thank Peter Fader, Shannon Berning, and Brett LoGiurato of Wharton School Press for their enthusiasm for the project and for their expertise and professionalism in shepherding the book through the publication process.

Notes

Introduction

1 Jason Dean, "Bezos Says Amazon Will Boost Investment in China," *Wall Street Journal*, June 6, 2007, https://www.wsj.com/articles/SB118101997012424647.

2 Karen Weise, "Amazon Gives Up on Chinese Domestic Shopping Business," *New York Times*, April 18, 2019, https://www.nytimes.com/2019/04/18/technology/amazon-china.html.

3 Noah Smith, "Who Has the World's No. 1 Economy? Not the U.S.," *Bloomberg*, October 18, 2017, https://www.bloomberg.com/opinion/articles/2017-10-18/who-has-the-world-s-no-1-economy-not-the-u-s.

4 Wikipedia, s.v. "List of Countries by GDP (PPP)," last modified June 15, 2020, https://en.wikipedia.org/wiki/List_of_countries_by_GDP_(PPP).

Chapter 1: This Is What a Business Needs to Succeed in China

1 Clayton M. Christensen, Taddy Hall, Karen Dillon, and David S. Duncan, "Know Your Customers' 'Jobs to Be Done,'" *Harvard Business Review*, September 2016, https://hbr.org/2016/09/know-your-customers-jobs-to-be-done.

2 China's Five Year Plan and other government resources.

3 Karl T. Ulrich, "Alpha Assets and Sustained Competitive Advantage" (working paper, Wharton School, University of Pennsylvania, 2020).

4 Harris Collingwood, "Do CEOs Matter?," *The Atlantic*, June 2009, https://www.theatlantic.com/magazine/archive/2009/06/do-ceos-matter/307437/.

Chapter 2: Amazon

1 Newley Purnell, "Jeff Bezos Invests Billions to Make Amazon a Top E-Commerce Player in India," *Wall Street Journal*, November 18, 2016, https://www.wsj.com/articles/bezos-invests-billions-to-make-amazon-a-top-e-commerce-player-in-india-1479384001.

2 Greg Bensinger, "Amazon Plans $3 Billion India Investment," *Wall Street Journal*, June 7, 2016, https://www.wsj.com/articles/amazon-plans-3-billion-india-investment-1465355857.

3 Liza Lin, "Why Amazon Isn't Ready for Prime Time in China," *Wall Street Journal*, August 27, 2017, https://www.wsj.com/articles/why-amazon-isnt-ready-for-prime-time-in-china-1503835204.

4   China Internet Network Information Center, "Statistical Report on Internet Development in China" [in Chinese], July 20, 2004, http://www.cnnic.cn/gywm /xwzx/rdxw/2004nrd/201207/t20120710_31395.htm.

5   iResearch, "China B2C Ecommerce Research Report 2005," May 12, 2006, http://www.iresearch.cn/include/ajax/user_ajax.ashx?work=idown&rid=533.

6   "China's Amazon," *The Economist*, August 21, 2003, https://www.economist.com /business/2003/08/21/chinas-amazon.

7   Gang Yu, interview by the authors, March 8, 2019. All subsequent quotes from Yu are from the same interview.

8   Matt Hines, "Amazon Buys Into Chinese Market," CNET, August 19, 2004, https://www.cnet.com/news/amazon-buys-into-chinese-market/.

9   Hines, "Amazon Buys Into Chinese Market."

10 Zhongshan Jia, "Taobao Transaction Broke 16.9 Billion Yuan" [in Chinese], Beijing Evening News, January 18, 2007, http://www.techweb.com.cn/news/2007 -01-18/143050.shtml; Liang Chen, "Taobao Takes 80% Share in C2C Market" [in Chinese], *Southern Daily*, April 17, 2007, http://www.techweb.com.cn/news/2007 -04-17/182651.shtml.

11 Former Amazon executive, interview by the authors, March 26, 2019. All subsequent quotes from the executive are from the same interview.

12 Former Amazon senior manager, interview by the authors, March 21, 2019. All subsequent quotes from the manager are from the same interview.

13 Shaoqing He, "Guoqing Li: Richard Liu Got $2 Billion to Burn" [in Chinese], Sohu.com, October 15, 2015, https://www.sohu.com/a/35934627_114812.

14 Melanie Lee, "Interview—Amazon Aims for Top Three in China Market," Reuters, May 10, 2012, https://www.reuters.com/article/amazon-china/interview -amazon-aims-for-top-three-in-china-market-idINDEE84907L20120510.

15 Vivienne Walt, "Amazon Invades India," *Fortune*, December 28, 2015, https:// fortune.com/longform/amazon-india-jeff-bezos/.

16 Yuntao Huang, "The Path to Profitability of Amazon China: A Marathon, Not a Sprint" [in Chinese], Reuters, May 17, 2012, https://www.reuters.com/article /amazon-cn-development-long-run-idCNCNE84G06E20120517.

17 Long Wong, interview by the authors, March 21, 2019. All subsequent quotes from Wong are from the same interview.

18 Liza Lin and Laura Stevens, "Why Amazon Isn't Ready for Prime Time in China," *Wall Street Journal*, August 27, 2017, https://www.wsj.com/articles/why -amazon-isnt-ready-for-prime-time-in-china-1503835204.

19 Yu Sun, "Amazon China: 'Everyday Low Price' e-tailer Doesn't Know How to Play Gimmicks" [in Chinese], *Talents Magazine*, March 12, 2013, http://finance .sina.com.cn/chanjing/gsnews/20130312/101614801972.shtml.

20 Kana Inagaki, "Amazon's Scale in Japan Challenges Rivals and Regulators," *Financial Times*, June 25, 2018, https://www.ft.com/content/f50c5f24-752f-11e8 -aa31-31da4279a601.

21 Lifen Wang, "How Richard Liu Thinks of His Competitors" [in Chinese], Youmi, 2011, YouTube video, 19:05, https://www.youtube.com/watch?v=fC_FxmkauLY.

Chapter 3: Norwegian Cruise Line

1 Carol Zhao, interview by the authors, September 28, 2019. All subsequent quotes from Zhao are from the same interview.

2 Monty Mathisen, "Del Rio: China Operation Is Profitable," Cruise Industry News, February 23, 2018, https://www.cruiseindustrynews.com/cruise-news /18570-del-rio-china-operation-is profitable.html.

3 Arnie Weissmann and Susan Li, "NCL's Frank Del Rio Talks China, Roast Chickens and Cardiac Surgeons," Travel Weekly Asia, March 30, 2016, https:// www.travelweekly-asia.com/Cruise-Travel/NCL-s-Frank-Del-Rio-talks-China -roast-chickens-and-cardiac-surgeons.

4 Jason Leppert, "Royal Caribbean International Takes Delivery of New Quantum of the Seas," Popular Cruising, October 30, 2014, https://popularcruising.com /royal-caribbean-international-takes-deliver-new-quantum-seas/.

5 Cheddar, "CEO of Norwegian Cruise Line Shares Secrets to Crack Chinese Market," Twitter, January 12, 2018, https://twitter.com/cheddar/status /951547404376981505?lang=en.

6 Jacintha Stephens, "Norwegian Joy Calls at Singapore en-route to China," Seatrade Cruise News, May 22, 2017, https://www.seatrade-cruise.com/news -headlines/norwegian-joy-calls-singapore-en-route-china.

7 Cruise Line International Association, *Asia Cruise Trends 2017 Edition*, July 2017, https://cruising.org/-/media/research-updates/research/asia-cruise -trends/asia-cruise-trends-2017.pdf.

8 Weihang Zheng, interview by the authors, October 30, 2019.

9 Alex Xiang, interview by the authors, September 22, 2019. All subsequent quotes from Xiang are from the same interview.

10 Laine Higgins, "How Norwegian Cruise's Chief Navigates the Sea-Suite," *Wall Street Journal*, February 22, 2019, https://www.wsj.com/articles/how-norwegian -cruises-chief-navigates-the-sea-suite-11550853001.

11 Frank Del Rio, "Out of Cuba, with a Suitcase," *New York Times*, June 11, 2011, https://www.nytimes.com/2011/06/12/jobs/12boss.html.

12 Jing Lin, interview by the authors, October 12, 2019. All subsequent quotes from Lin are from the same interview.

13 Hannah Walhout, "Goodbye Tea Room, Hello Brew Pub—How to Move a Cruise Ship from China to the Americas," *Travel+Leisure*, June 10, 2019,

https://www.travelandleisure.com/cruises/norwegian-joy-cruise-ship
-renovation-china-americas.

Chapter 4: Hyundai

1 Hyuk Joon Lee, interview by the authors, August 29, 2019. All subsequent
   quotes from Lee are from the same interview.

2 Rose Yu, "Chinese Cars Fall Farther Behind," *Wall Street Journal*, February 22,
   2015, https://www.wsj.com/articles/chinese-cars-fall-farther-behind
   -1424644382.

3 Ning Zhu, interview by the authors, August 30, 2019.

4 Dongshu Cui, interview by the authors, September 22, 2019.

5 China Central Television, "ShuFu Li: Turning the Impossible into a Miracle" [in
   Chinese], April 8, 2019, YouTube video, 42:40, https://www.youtube.com/watch
   ?v=AV9cSCGv55M.

6 Volvo Global Newsroom, "Volvo Cars Goes from Strength to Strength as First
   V90 Rolls Off Production Line," June 22, 2016, https://www.media.volvocars
   .com/global/en-gb/media/pressreleases/193246/volvo-cars-goes-from-strength
   -to-strength-as-first-v90-rolls-off-production-line.

7 China Central Television, "ShuFu Li: Turning the Impossible into a Miracle."

8 Robert Bao, interview by the authors, November 11, 2019. All subsequent
   quotes from Bao are from the same interview.

9 China Central Television, "ShuFu Li: Turning the Impossible into a Miracle."

10 Dengfeng He, "Hyundai Speed Accelerates Beijing's Economical Growth" [in
   Chinese], *Beijing Youth Daily*, October 20, 2003, http://finance.sina.com.cn/roll
   /20031020/0432480994.shtml.

11 Shuyuan Zhou, "Hainachuan Fights Against Mobis" [in Chinese], *China
   Business Journal*, March 27, 2010, http://finance.ifeng.com/roll/20100327
   /1974976.shtml.

12 Xiaodong Zhang, "Beijing Hyundai: Low Profit and Weak Brand" [in Chinese],
   Economic Observer, December 27, 2008, http://auto.sina.com.cn/news/2008-12
   -27/0928444490.shtml.

13 William Xu, interview by the authors, November 10, 2019. All subsequent
   quotes from Xu are from the same interview.

14 Gang Cong, "Hexi Xu Aims to Break Mobis Monopoly" [in Chinese], *21 Century
   Business Herald*, July 23, 2007, http://auto.sohu.com/20070723/n251193868
   .shtml.

15 Weigang Chen, interview by the authors, November 15, 2019.

16 Yoko Kubota and Kentaro Sugiyama, "China's Demand for Japanese Cars Has
   Collapsed," Reuters, October 8, 2012, https://www.businessinsider.com/japan
   -car-production-slashed-in-china-2012-10.

17 Jonathan Soble, "Toyota and Honda Post Record China Sales," *Financial Times*, January 7, 2014, https://www.ft.com/content/e79a64bc-76b0-11e3-a253 -00144feabdc0.

Chapter 5: LinkedIn

1 Derek Shen, "Chitu Went Offline—What's the Future for China's Professional Networking," WeChat official account, June 26, 2019.

2 LinkedIn executive, interview by the author, December 13, 2019. All subsequent quotes from the executive are from the same interview.

3 In the Loop, "Jeff Weiner: LinkedIn's Expansion into China Is Key," Bloomberg TV, October 10, 2014, https://www.bloomberg.com/news/videos/2014-10-10 /linkedin-ceo-learned-a-lot-by-expanding-into-china.

4 In the Loop, "Jeff Weiner."

5 Linus Chung, interview by the author, January 30, 2019. All subsequent quotes from Chung are from the same interview.

6 Mark Feng, interview by the author, December 12, 2018.

7 Derek Shen, "The Backstory of LinkedIn's Offline Ads" [in Chinese], jiemian .com, June 12, 2015, https://www.jiemian.com/article/302880.html.

8 Robin Zhang, interview by the author, November 30, 2018. All subsequent quotes from Zhang are from the same interview.

9 Yanan Liu, "Derek Shen: How I Built a Startup within LinkedIn" [in Chinese], Tencent News, July 8, 2015, https://tech.qq.com/a/20150708/007762 .htm.

10 Shuting Zhong and Junjie Huang, "Why LinkedIn Isn't Enough and How Chitu Comes to Life" [in Chinese], qdaily.com, July 27, 2015, http://www.qdaily.com /articles/12619.html.

11 Zongshen Cai, "Derek Shen: LinkedIn's Advantage Lies in Its 400 Million Users" [in Chinese], the Paper, June 15, 2016, https://www.thepaper.cn/newsDetail _forward_1484158.

12 Neil Shen, interview by the authors, June 21, 2019.

13 Paul Mozur and Carolyn Zhang, "In China, Silicon Valley Giants Confront New Walls," *New York Times*, July 22, 2017, https://www.nytimes.com/2017/07 /22/technology/in-china-silicon-valley-giants-confront-new-walls.html?_ga=2 .103634626.397406077.1591088213-2146251008.1557009184.

14 Derek Shen, "So Long, LinkedIn" [in Chinese], LinkedIn, June 23, 2017, https://www.linkedin.com/pulse/再见领英-derek-shen/.

Chapter 6: Sequoia Capital

1 Doug Leone, interview by the author, June 21, 2019. All subsequent quotes from Leone are from the same interview.

2   Neil Shen, interview by the author, June 21, 2019. All subsequent quotes from Shen are from the same interview.

3   Charlie Cambell, "Lei Jun Wants to Be China's Answer to Steve Jobs. But Trump's Trade War Is Getting in His Way," *Time*, July 12, 2018, https://time.com/5336633/lei-jun-xiaomi-trade-war/.

4   Julia Fioretti and Donny Kwok, "Tencent-Backed Meituan Climbs 5 Percent on Debut, Brightens Outlook for HK IPOs," Reuters, September 19, 2018, https://www.reuters.com/article/us-meituan-listing/tencent-backed-meituan-climbs-5-percent-on-debut-brightens-outlook-for-hk-ipos-idUSKCN1M00CK.

5   Xiaopeng He, "Predict the Future" [in Chinese] (speech at Yabuli China Entrepreneurs Forum, Hong Kong, June 15, 2019), https://finance.sina.com.cn/hy/hyjz/2019-06-15/doc-ihvhiqay5898429.shtml.

6   Xing Wang, "My Ten Years with Sequoia" [in Chinese] (speech at Sequoia China 10-year anniversary ceremony, October 17, 2015), http://news.sina.com.cn/o/2015-10-23/doc-ifxizetf7974748.shtml.

7   Udayan Gupta, *Done Deals: Venture Capitalists Tell Their Stories* (Boston: Harvard Business School Press, 2000).

8   Udayan Gupta, *Done Deals*.

9   Xing Wang, "My Ten Years with Sequoia."

10 Tao Zhang, interview by the authors, June 30, 2019.

11 Xing Liu, interview by the authors, June 25, 2020.

12 Xing Liu, interview by authors, March 11, 2019.

Chapter 7: InMobi

1   Jessie Yang, interview by the authors, November 23, 2019. All subsequent quotes are from the same interview.

2   Naveen Tewari, interview by the authors, November 8, 2019. All subsequent quotes are from the same interview.

3   Xiyuan Zhang, "China's Mobile Phone Users Broke 900 Million" [in Chinese], People.com.cn, May 25, 2011, http://media.people.com.cn/GB/40606/14728823.html.

4   Kevin Wang, interview by the authors, November 26, 2019. All subsequent quotes are from the same interview.

5   Yangwu Huiying, "Making Ads No Longer Annoying" [in Chinese], *YiMagazine*, September 2, 2015, https://weibo.com/p/1001603882641957990907.

Chapter 8: Intel

1   Bin Xia and Cheng Xu, "Ian Yang: Wining the Future with China" [in Chinese], China News Service, September 24, 2019, https://finance.sina.com.cn/stock/relnews/us/2019-09-24/doc-iicezzrq8082290.shtml.

2   Don Clark, "Intel's Culture Needed Fixing. Its C.E.O. Is Shaking Things Up," *New York Times*, March 1, 2020, https://www.nytimes.com/2020/03/01 /technology/intel-culture-robert-swan.html.

3   Dean Takahashi, "AST Will Build $16-Million PC Plant in China," *Los Angeles Times*, September 8, 1993, https://www.latimes.com/archives/la-xpm-1993-09 -08-fi-32953-story.html; Sina Tech, "IBM Plans to Move Asia Pacific Headquarters from Japan to Shanghai" [in Chinese], Sina.com, January 8, 2004, http://tech.sina.com.cn/it/2004-01-08/1835279617.shtml; Associated Press, "China Plant for Motorola," *New York Times*, March 28, 1992, https://www .nytimes.com/1992/03/28/business/china-plant-for-motorola.html; Xiang Huang, "Zhengyao Sun Talks about HP and the China Market" [in Chinese], *Fortune China*, March 1, 2004, https://www.fortunechina.com/magazine/c/2004 -03/01/content_845.htm.

4   National Bureau of Statistics of China, "Opening Up" [in Chinese], September 11, 2009, http://www.gov.cn/test/2009-09/11/content_1415347_5.htm.

5   Wee Theng Tan, *Embedded: Intel in China: The Inside Story* (Singapore: Marshall Cavendish Corporation, 2010).

6   Wee Theng Tan, interview by the authors, March 12, 2019. All subsequent quotes are from the same interview.

7   Zhijun Ling, *The Lenovo Affair* (Beijing: CITIC Press Group, 2005).

8   Zhichao Dong Shicheng and Nong Xiang, "Why Has Intel Been Paranoid" [in Chinese], *IT Times Weekly*, October 24, 2005, http://tech.sina.com.cn/it/2005-10 -24/1034746377.shtml.

9   Wee Theng Tan, *Embedded*.

10   Wangli Moser, interview by the authors, March 16, 2019.

11   Cheng Chen, "Honglin Ge: IT Industry in Chengdu Dates Back to 1950s" [in Chinese], *21st Century Business Herald*, January 19, 2012, http://www.weste.net /2012/1-19/79347.html.

12   Noel Randewich and Matthew Miller, "Qualcomm to Pay $975 Million to Resolve China Antitrust Dispute," Reuters, February 10, 2015, https://www .reuters.com/article/us-china-qualcomm/qualcomm-to-pay-975-million-to -resolve-china-antitrust-dispute-idUSKBN0LD2EL20150210.

13   Wee Theng Tan, *Embedded*; "China Becomes Biggest PC Market in 2012—IHS report," BBC, April 29, 2013, https://www.bbc.com/news/business-22346821; interview with Tan by the authors.

14   Intel annual report 2017 and 2018.

15   Gordon Orr and Christopher Thomas, "Semiconductors in China: Brave New World or Same Old Story?," Mckinsey.com, August 1, 2014, https://www .mckinsey.com/industries/semiconductors/our-insights/semiconductors-in -china-brave-new-world-or-same-old-story.

16 Yimou Lee, "China Lures Chip Talent from Taiwan with Fat Salaries, Perks," Reuters, September 4, 2018, https://www.reuters.com/article/us-china-semiconductors-taiwan-insight/china-lures-chip-talent-from-taiwan-with-fat-salaries-perks-idUSKCN1LK0H1.

17 R&D leader at Intel, interview by the authors, May 25, 2019. All subsequent quotes are from the same interview.

18 Stacey Higginbotham, "Secrets of Intel's 'Super 7' Cloud Computing Customers," *Fortune*, November 15, 2015, https://fortune.com/2015/11/15/intel-super-7/.

Chapter 9: Zegna

1 Peter Marino, "Gildo Zegna," *Interview Magazine*, April 27, 2010, https://www.interviewmagazine.com/fashion/gildo-zegna.

2 Georgina Safe, "Zegna Keeps It in the Family to Expand Its Retail Empire," *Sydney Morning Herald*, September 22, 2011, https://www.smh.com.au/lifestyle/zegna-keeps-it-in-the-family-to-expand-its-retail-empire-20110921-1klbu.html.

3 Safe, "Zegna Keeps It in the Family."

4 Radha Chadha and Paul Husband, *Cult of the Luxury Brand: Inside Asia's Love Affair with Luxury* (Boston: Nicholas Brealey, 2010).

5 Annie Hou, interview by the authors, April 22, 2020. All subsequent quotes from Hou are from the same interview.

6 Wenbin Wu, interview by the authors, May 10, 2020.

7 Thomas Gorman, "Building Strong Family Business: Interview with Zegna CEO Gildo Zegna" [in Chinese], *Fortune* (China), November 16, 2009, http://www.fortunechina.com/magazine/c/2009-11/16/content_26792.htm.

8 Inge Hufschlag Handelsblatt, "Italian Designer Zegna Seeks to Suit Men at Home, Office," *Wall Street Journal*, February 18, 2000, https://www.wsj.com/articles/SB950811022503451772.

9 Former boutique manager, interview by the authors, April 17, 2020.

10 Chen Qin, "Beyond the Brand" [in Chinese], *Fortune* (China), October 15, 2011, http://www.fortunechina.com/management/c/2011-10/15/content_74960.htm.

11 Chen Qin, "Beyond the Brand."

12 Sally Stiegler, interview by the authors, May 22, 2020.

13 Former executive, interview by the authors, April 27, 2020. All subsequent quotes from the executive are from the same interview.

14 Laurie Burkitt, "Fashion House Zegna Battles Rivals for China's Affluent," *Wall Street Journal*, September 15, 2011, https://www.wsj.com/articles/SB10001424053111903927204576570561308825184.

15 Bain & Company, *2011 China Luxury Market Study*, December 2011, https://media.bain.com/Images/2011%20Bain%20China%20Luxury%20Market%20Study.pdf.

16   Chris Buckley, "China's Leader Wears Many Hats, but Only One Jacket," *New York Times*, May 25, 2016, https://www.nytimes.com/2016/05/26/world/asia /china-president-xi-jinping-windbreaker.html.

17   Buckley, "China's Leader Wears Many Hats."

18   Bain & Company, *2017 China Luxury Market Study*, January 2018, http://www .bain.com.cn/pdfs/201801180441238002.pdf.

19   Ogilvy China, "Making Luxury Brands Matter," April 2019, https://www.ogilvy .com.cn/2019-luxury-report/full-en.pdf.

20   Ben Bland, "Zegna Tailors Strategy for Changing Chinese Market," *Financial Times*, October 8, 2015, https://www.ft.com/content/39b0224a-6da5-11e5-aca9 -d87542bf8673.

21   Zhizhong Du, interview by the author, April 22, 2020.

22   Elizabeth Segran, "How a Century-Old Luxury Brand Like Gucci Won Over Gen Z," Fast Company, July 10, 2019, https://www.fastcompany.com/90374520 /how-a-century-old-luxury-brand-like-gucci-won-over-gen-z.

23   Lucy Handley, "Instagram Could Be a Crucial Stock-Picking Tool When Investing in Luxury Firms," CNBC, October 19, 2018, https://www.cnbc.com/2018/10/19 /luxury-brands-instagram-likes-could-be-crucial-for-stock-picking.html.

24   McKinsey & Company, *China Luxury Report 2019*, April 2019, https://www .mckinsey.com/~/media/mckinsey/featured%20insights/china/how%20 young%20chinese%20consumers%20are%20reshaping%20global%20luxury /mckinsey-china-luxury-report-2019-how-young-chinese-consumers-are -reshaping-global-luxury.ashx.

25   Michelle Toh, "Chinese Shoppers Are Giving Luxury Brands Some Hope," CNN, June 11, 2020, https://www.cnn.com/2020/06/11/business/global-luxury-sales -china-coronavirus-intl-hnk/index.html.

26   Tianwei Zhang, "Hermès Hauled in $2.7 Million in One China Store on Saturday: Sources," WWD, April 13, 2020, https://wwd.com/fashion-news /fashion-scoops/hermes-hauled-in-2-7-million-in-one-china-store-on-saturday -sources-1203559738/.

Chapter 11: Prescriptions for Success

1   Theodore Levitt, "Marketing Myopia," *Harvard Business Review* 38, no. 4 (1960): 45–56.

2   Christian Terwiesch and Karl Ulrich, *Innovation Tournaments: Creating and Selecting Exceptional Opportunities* (Boston: Harvard Business Press, 2009).

3   Terwiesch and Ulrich, *Innovation Tournaments*.

4   Bain & Company, "RAPID®: Bain's Tool to Clarify Decision Accountability," August 11, 2011, https://www.bain.com/insights/rapid-tool-to-clarify-decision -accountability/#:~:text=To%20address%20this%20common%20problem, key%20roles%20in%20any%20decision.

5 David Robertson and Karl Ulrich, "Planning for Product Platforms," *Sloan Management Review* 39, no. 4 (1998): 19–31.

Conclusion

1 Yoko Kubota, "China Chases Foreign Capital to Fend Off Coronavirus Slowdown," *Wall Street Journal*, April 9, 2020, https://www.wsj.com/articles /china-chases-foreign-capital-to-fend-off-coronavirus-slowdown-11586430003.

2 Wikipedia, s.v. "May You Live in Interesting Times," last modified on June 3, 2020, https://en.wikipedia.org/wiki/May_you_live_in_interesting_times.

Index

Page references ending with a t indicate a table.

About the Authors

Lele Sang is a global fellow at the Wharton School of the University of Pennsylvania. A former journalist and editor, she has worked for the *Beijing News* and *Caijing Magazine* covering business and politics. She was also a visiting scholar at UC Berkeley, Graduate School of Journalism. She holds an MPA degree from the University of Pennsylvania.

Karl T. Ulrich is vice dean of entrepreneurship and innovation at the Wharton School of the University of Pennsylvania. His recent work focuses on innovation strategy, with a particular emphasis on innovation in China. He is the coauthor of *Product Design and Development* (7th ed., McGraw-Hill, 2019) and of *Innovation Tournaments* (Harvard Business Press, 2009). Ulrich holds bachelor's, master's, and doctoral degrees in mechanical engineering from MIT.

About Wharton School Press

Wharton School Press, the book publishing arm of the Wharton School of the University of Pennsylvania, was established to inspire bold, insightful thinking within the global business community.

Wharton School Press publishes a select list of award-winning, best-selling, and thought-leading books that offer trusted business knowledge to help leaders at all levels meet the challenges of today and the opportunities of tomorrow. Led by a spirit of innovation and experimentation, Wharton School Press leverages groundbreaking digital technologies and has pioneered a fast-reading business book format that fits readers' busy lives, allowing them to swiftly emerge with the tools and information needed to make an impact. Wharton School Press books offer guidance and inspiration on a variety of topics, including leadership, management, strategy, innovation, entrepreneurship, finance, marketing, social impact, public policy, and more.

Wharton School Press also operates an online bookstore featuring a curated selection of influential books by Wharton School faculty and Press authors published by a wide range of leading publishers.

To find books that will inspire and empower you to increase your impact and expand your personal and professional horizons, visit *wsp.wharton.upenn.edu.*

About the Wharton School

Founded in 1881 as the world's first collegiate business school, the Wharton School of the University of Pennsylvania is shaping the future of business by incubating ideas, driving insights, and creating leaders who change the world. With a faculty of more than 235 renowned professors, Wharton has 5,000 undergraduate, MBA, executive MBA, and doctoral students. Each year 18,000 professionals from around the world advance their careers through Wharton Executive Education's individual, company-customized, and online programs. More than 99,000 Wharton alumni form a powerful global network of leaders who transform business every day.

www.wharton.upenn.edu